Vintage & Historic
STOCK CARS

Dr. John Craft

Motorbooks International
Publishers & Wholesalers ®

Acknowledgments

This book would not have been possible without the much appreciated help of:
Don Namon, Director, International Motorsports Hall of Fame, Talladega, Alabama;
Meta Haynie, Joe Weatherly Stock Car Racing Museum, Darlington, South Carolina;
Alex Beam, Davidson, North Carolina; Mike Slade, Rock Hill, South Carolina;
and Kim Haynes, Gastonia, North Carolina.

First published in 1994 by Motorbooks International Publishers & Wholesalers, PO Box 2, 729 Prospect Avenue, Osceola, WI 54020 USA

Motorbooks International books are also available at discounts in bulk quantity for industrial or sales-promotional use. For details write to Special Sales Manager at the Publisher's address

Printed in Hong Kong

Library of Congress Cataloging-in-Publication Data

Craft, John Albert.
    Vintage & historic stock cars / John Craft.
       p.   cm. – (Enthusiast color series)
    Includes index.
    ISBN 0-87938-898-6
      1. Automobiles, Racing–United States–History.
2. Stock car racing–United States–History. I. Title.
II. Title: Vintage and historic stock cars. III. Series.
    TL236.C694   1994
    796.7'2'0973–dc20   93-48645

On the front cover: The most widely recognized stock cars in the world surely are those that have been driven by Richard Petty. This 1972 Dodge Charger sports Petty blue paint and the familiar logos of his long-time sponsors.

On the frontispiece: Body panels have always served as billboards in stock car racing. The oddly styled bulging fenders of mid-seventies Monte Carlos provides ample room for display of sponsors' and contingency stickers.

On the title page: The "aero wars" era in NASCAR racing featured cars such as this 1969 Ford Torino Talladega driven by Donnie Allison. Although not as radical as their winged Mopar competition, Talladegas were the winningest aero warriors during the 1969 and 1970 NASCAR seasons.

On the back cover: While 1964 Galaxies were large, the driver of this particular one was tiny, Tiny Lund, that is. Note that Grand National cars of the era still sported full factory glass and all manner of assembly line brightwork.

Contents

Introduction

NASCAR Winston Cup (nee Grand National) racing has become the most popular form of motorsports in the United States. And that's easy to understand. Twenty-nine times every year forty-plus cars roll out to battle at a track on the circuit. What happens next can't accurately be described to those who have not actually witnessed the spectacle for themselves, first hand. It is equal parts noise, color, speed and close-quarters action. And it is called stock car racing.

The word stock actually has little relevance to the goings on at a contemporary NASCAR track, though it once did. In fact, when "Big" Bill France presided over the very first NASCAR race in 1949, the cars on that Charlotte Speedway starting grid actually were stock enough for their drivers to have driven them to the racetrack—and some of them did. As the series matured and speeds rose, an increasing number of modifications began to show up in the Grand National garage area.

At first those changes took the form of safety improvements. But it wasn't long before major auto makers noticed the sales activity that NASCAR wins on Sunday generated on the showroom floor Monday morning. Shortly thereafter, special "export" high-performance racing components began to show up in those manufacturers' official parts books. That trend escalated throughout the fifties and sixties until by 1969, the major auto manufacturers were actually building special engines and even whole cars specifically for use on the NASCAR circuit.

Modern Winston Cup stock cars have very little in common with their erstwhile showroom counterparts. Though seemingly "stock" in appearance, the cars that Dale Earnhardt and Bill Elliott campaign have never seen the inside of a UAW assembly plant. Instead, they all started life as an odd collection of tubular steel and sheet stock in a fabricator's shop. It is only after countless manhours and repeated trips to the wind tunnel that there begins to be any resemblance between those bits and pieces of metal and a showroom-new Thunderbird or Lumina.

This book is a photographic attempt to trace the evolution of the NASCAR Grand National/Winston Cup stock car. The cars pictured here include both real race cars that were lucky enough to survive their days of "rubbing fenders" on the track, and recreations of those that didn't. Truth be known, precious few of the cars that were campaigned on the circuit in its first three decades have survived. Racing is a generally unsentimental activity where last season's chassis is quickly sold or discarded the moment its usefulness has ended. The passing of those cars into oblivion makes it successively harder for each new generation of NASCAR fans to recall the early days of the series.

This book's goal is to help the millions of fans who have come only lately to the sport understand its roots. And, perhaps, to introduce them for the first time to early NASCAR stars like Glenn "Fireball" Roberts, Tim Flock, Herb Thomas, and Fred Lorenzen by way of the cars they drove.

Those already well acquainted with NASCAR's earliest days will hopefully find their recollections of those formative years refreshed by revisiting the Mystery Motor

Impalas, Hudson Hornets, and Torino Talladegas that vied for the Grand National Championship in seasons long past.

Along with the photos and text that portray each race car in this volume, the reader will find as a point of reference, a short list of each car's technical specifications. Among them is the qualifying speed for the Southern 500 at Darlington (the only track to host all of the assembled cars) during the years each was in competition.

Here's an historic car: Alan Kulwicki in his Thunderbird that bears the colors of the US Army to show support for the Desert Storm troops.

Vintage and Historic Stock Cars

BUCK BAKER'S 1950 OLDSMOBILE

Though contemporary ad campaigns might suggest otherwise, your father's Oldsmobile *was* literally a rocket. Which is why it was so aptly called the Rocket 88. The secret of the car's speed was General Motors' (GM) all new overhead valve, 303 cubic inch (ci) V-8 that was introduced in 1949. Lightweight "slipper" pistons, high compression, and the all-important valve-in-head configuration added up to high horsepower. Installed in a light-for-the-times 3,600 pound (lb) Rocket 88 full-frame chassis, the new package was the fastest Detroit iron available to the public.

That was of no small significance to racers on Big Bill France's fledgling "Strictly Stock" circuit. The NASCAR rules book of the period allowed precious few modifications to the two-door sedans sanctioned for competition. Consequently, a car's showroom stock performance capabilities were of prime importance. Drivers like Fireball Roberts, Buck Baker, Tim Flock, and Curtis Turner used the Rocket 88's high speed capability to expeditiously negotiate the dirt and asphalt tracks of the day. In fact, in the first Southern 500 at Darlington, South Carolina, in 1950, nearly half of the seventy-five car field (that's right, seventy-five cars vied for track position in NASCAR's first superspeedway race!) consisted of Rocket 88s.

Among them was a car driven by Buck Baker similar to the one currently on display in the Joe Weatherly Stock Car Muse-

Though clumsy and ungainly by contemporary standards, Rocket 88 Oldsmobiles were the cars to beat on the NASCAR circuit in the early fifties. The rules book in 1950 precluded most modifications, save those made for safety purposes. As a result, drivers were more than a little interested in the power-to-weight ratio of each model year's new cars. In 1950, Oldsmobile Rocket 88s were the fastest production vehicles made in America, and they quickly found their way into the winner's circle on NASCAR tracks all across the southeast. *Mike Slade*

1950 OLDSMOBILE
Wheelbase: 119.5in
Weight: 3,600lb
Suspension: "A" frames/live axle
Brakes: Drums
Engine: 303ci, ohv V-8, 135hp
Transmission: Three-speed manual/factory
Speed at Darlington: 82.03mph

um, trackside in Darlington. Baker's rocket ship wasn't that far removed from its assembly line configuration. The chassis rolled on live axle rear and independent front suspension and relied on drum brakes to slow it from the 70-80mph velocities typical at big tracks like Darlington. A spindly looking roll cage provided a modicum of protection. The 135 horse (hp) V-8 under

Race cars really were stock in the early days of Grand National Competition. Though passenger seats (or seat backs) could be removed and rudimentary roll cages (sometimes constructed of 2 x 4s!) were permitted, the cockpit of a race car like Buck Baker's 1950 Olds was mostly assembly line original.

the massive hood was backed by a stock clutch and factory three-speed manual transmission. Running at full chat, that drivetrain hauled Curtis "Pops" Turner around the "Lady in Black's" banked surface at a pole-setting 82.03mph in 1950. Though slow by modern standards, that speed was sufficient to make Rocket 88s the most successful cars on the track in the early fifties. During NASCAR Grand National seasons from 1949-59, Olds drivers won eighty-six races and two Grand National Championships. Your father's Oldsmobile, indeed!

HERB THOMAS' 1951 HUDSON HORNET

The concept of aerodynamics was as foreign to the auto industry in the forties and fifties as modesty is to Madonna today. Cars of that era were generally as sleek and trim as your average brick, and their performance suffered as a result—both on and off the racetrack. The Hudson automobile company literally changed the shape of the automotive world in the early fifties when it began designing cars with aerodynamics in mind. The Hudson Hornet was the result of that focus. Though powered by turgid flathead, in-line six-cylinder engines, Hornets slipped through the air with so little drag that they were still some of the fastest cars on the road.

Racers like Herb Thomas quickly recognized the Hornet's potential for winning NASCAR races, and Hudson helped by offering "factory stock" horsepower add-ons that were clearly designed for one purpose: Grand National competition. The "Twin H Power" dual carburetor option helped wake up the Hornet's sleepy, valve-

The secret of the Rocket 88's success on the NASCAR circuit was found beneath the car's massive stock hood. Introduced in 1949, the new 303ci ohv that powered the Olds Rocket line was both powerful and lightweight. After taking a back seat to Ford V-8 drivers for seventeen years, GM hot shoes quickly put the new V-8 engine in victory lane.

A 1951 Hudson Hornet would no doubt suffer in any comparison of sleekness with even the meanest of modern econoboxes. Be that as it may, cars like Herb Thomas' Fabulous Hudson represented the cutting edge of automotive aerodynamics when Harry

Truman was still playing the piano at 1600 Pennsylvania Avenue. Note the full trim and roll-up windows that made wreck cleanup a protracted affair in the early days of Grand National competition. *Mike Slade*

11

in-block, 308ci engine. Other thinly disguised "racer" options included "export" axle ratios. Over-the-counter availability and bonafide factory parts numbers made the new components "legal" for competition in NASCAR's eyes, and Hornets became consistent winners.

Early NASCAR star Herb Thomas piloted a Hornet similar to the Joe Weatherly Stock Car Museum replica shown here to seven Grand National victories in 1951.

Fabulous Hudson drivers in the next three seasons racked up sixty-six more GN victories and two more national driving championships (by Tim Flock in 1952 and a second one for Thomas in 1953).

Along with winning races and reshaping industry views on aerodynamics, Hudsons also indirectly contributed to the trend away from stock configuration in NASCAR racing due to their tendency to break rear axles. A broken axle in a Hudson's nearly enclosed wheel very often led to a trapped rim and tire, a horrendous flip, and serious driver injuries—in that order. As a result, NASCAR officials soon allowed the use of "floating" axles derived from Ford trucks. Wrecks caused by broken axles became a thing of the past, as did the notion of strictly stock NASCAR competition.

1951 HUDSON HORNET
Wheelbase: 124in
Weight: 3,600lb
Suspension: "A" frames/live axle
Brakes: Drums and shoes
Engine: 308ci valve-in-block I-6, 210hp
Transmission: Column-shifted,
   three-speed manual
Speed at Darlington: 87.636mph

BUCK BAKER'S 1956 CHRYSLER 300

The garage area of a typical NASCAR race in the fifties was characterized by open car trailers (in the earliest days competitors drove their race cars to the track!), tailgate picnic lunches, and single-car teams. Imagine the impact, then, made by Mercury Marine President Carl Kiekhaefer when he burst onto the NASCAR scene in 1955 with: a trio of race cars housed in enclosed, long-haul trucks; a squadron of drivers and mechanics; and even a team of soil and weather experts who gave advice on dirt track tire selection and carburetor jetting.

Kiekhaefer, a hard-nosed businessman, had decided race victories by teams sponsored by his outboard boat motor company were the quickest way to increased sales. His professional approach to scoring those wins set the NASCAR world on its ear.

Kiekhaefer chose the new-for-1955 Chrysler 300 line as the instrument for those victories, primarily because it had the most powerful non-supercharged engine ever offered in an American car. Each of the 300-horse team cars was immaculately prepared and was campaigned by the best drivers and mechanics available. Tim Flock won eighteen of thirty-two races the team entered its first year on the circuit and snared the GN driving championship.

For 1956, Chrysler introduced a new "Fire Power" Hemi-headed engine that had been punched out to 354ci. It came factory equipped with two four-barrel carburetors, high-compression pistons, and a high-performance camshaft. In peak tune, the engine produced more than one horsepower per cubic inch—a first in the American automotive industry. Kiekhaefer's 1956

On the street, Chrysler's 300 series was the last word in personal high-speed transport. The same can be said of their racing counterparts. When stripped of their luxury accoutrements and dressed in Mercury Outboard racing livery, Kiekhaefer's B300s became the masters of just about every racing grid they graced. Racing rules of the day required full factory glass and the retention of most original brightwork. "Bungie" cords kept hoods and trunk lids in place during competition. *Mike Slade*

1956 CHRYSLER 300
Wheelbase: 126in
Weight: 4,005lb
Suspension: Independent "A" frames, coil springs, air bags and twin shocks per wheel (front); live axle leaf springs, twin shocks per wheel (rear).
Brakes: Reinforced/ventilated drums
Engine: 354ci, hemispherically headed ohv, dual 4V, V-8, 355hp.
Transmission: Column-shifted, three-speed manual
Speed at Darlington: 118.683mph

Tim Flock's M335 must have looked very stock indeed to the fans in the grandstands during the 1957 GN season. Truth be known, it was anything but. Factory backed racing that year produced a parts book full of "legal" high-performance parts that were exclusively intended for NASCAR use. Their part numbers, just like the still-required chrome trim, were all a ruse to conceal the car's true purpose-built nature. *Mike Slade*

B300s used column-shifted three-speed manual transmissions, live axle differentials, and a full-framed chassis that had received several "legal" suspension and braking upgrades.

Kiekhaefer fielded a new three-driver team of Buck Baker, Herb Thomas, and Speedy Thompson. Each was a star, and each received a star's salary: $40,000 a year, an incredible amount in 1956. Team drivers won thirty of fifty events entered, including sixteen consecutive races in one stretch, and Buck Baker was the year's GN driving champion. Unfortunately for Kiekhaefer, his racing success (fifty-two wins in ninety starts in 1955 and 1956) did not produce the positive publicity and sales he hoped for. In fact, his team's total dominance on the circuit generated quite the opposite reaction.

This example of a Kiekhaefer B300 currently belongs to Jack Boxstrom of Sebring, Florida.

TIM FLOCK'S 1957 MERCURY

With few exceptions, the Ford Motor Company's Lincoln Mercury division has seldom been associated with motorsports competition. Even so, Lincoln Mercury race cars have at times dominated their on-track rivals. For example, after the very first NASCAR race in June 1949, Jim Roper's Lincoln was the car in Charlotte Speedway's victory lane. In the fifties, Left Coast racer Bill Stroppe built a fleet of 1957 M335 Mercurys for Tim Flock, Jim Paschal, and Billy Myers to counter Holman & Moody's factory backed Ford operation.

Though based on assembly line Mercury sedans, "stock" cars like the Flock replica housed in the International Motorsports Hall of Fame Museum in Talladega, Alabama, sported all manner of modifications. Suspension members were substantially reinforced, for example, and four shock absorbers were mounted per wheel. Braking was improved by reinforcing the shoes and ventilating their mounting plates. Special racing rubber was introduced in the late fifties and those stronger-than-stock tires were mounted on reinforced rims.

Under the hood, two four-barrel carburetors, an aluminum intake manifold, forged steel truck crank, high-compression pistons, and an "Isky" hot rod cam that conveniently carried a Mercury part number all helped the 368ci "Y" block engine produce 335hp. Hence the M335 designation. A column-shifted truck transmission mounted behind a Cragar aluminum bell housing and HD truck clutch rounded out the running gear and transmitted torque to a truck-derived "full floater" live axle.

Full shoulder harnesses with quick-release, aircraft-derived mounts were now

1957 MERCURY
Wheelbase: 118in
Weight: 4,069lb
Suspension: Reinforced "A" frames, coils, air bags, two shocks per wheel (front); HD leaf springs, live axle and two shocks per wheel (rear)
Engine: 368 ci, ohv, dual 4V, V-8, 335hp
Transmission: Column-shifted, three-speed manual
Speed at Darlington: 117mph

standard and the 2 x 4 roll cages of earlier days had been replaced by a significantly sturdier collection of tubing.

Fewer than 100 street-going M335 Mercurys were built in 1957, which clearly underlines the fact that Flock's car was a purpose-built race car thinly disguised with spurious parts numbers. But, what the heck? Stroppe's cars were up against fuel-injected Chevrolets and supercharged Fords that were just as far removed from stock configuration.

The upshot of these "legal" modifications was that speeds rose and lap times fell. By 1957 it took 117.416mph to sit on the pole in the Southern 500, and top speeds in qualifying were just a tick short of the 120 mark.

JIM REED'S 1959 CHEVROLET

Chevrolet's modern success in Winston Cup (nee Grand National) competition stands in stark contrast to that marque's near total absence from stock car racing during NASCAR's formative years. GM's Bow Tie division did not notch its first official victory on a NASCAR track until Herb

Most of the original Impala dash and interior appointments remained in place. That included the stock bench seat. Aftermarket gauges were used in place of their less accurate OEM counterparts, however, and the stock rim was heavily wrapped with tape to improve grip. Note the white lanyard just visible in the right side of the frame. It is attached to a floorboard-mounted trap door that could be raised (via the lanyard) during the race to visually inspect the tread of the right front tire. Tire failure was a common occurrence in NASCAR's early days.

Left
The styling of Jim Reed's 1959 Impala stocker reflected the nation's fondness for wings in the late fifties. On Reed's 348 powered stock car, those wings helped him to "fly" to an upset victory over many better known GN drivers in the 1959 Southern 500. Though the rules book of the day did permit headlight buckets to be fared over, most of the bits and pieces of the Impala's original brightwork remained in place. Note the diagonal cross bracing of the roll cage that had become part of the increasingly more sophisticated NASCAR roll cage by 1959. *Mike Slade*

Thomas won the 1955 Southern 500 at Darlington in a Smokey Yunick-prepared "Motoramic" Chevrolet. Chevrolet's racing fortunes steadily improved thereafter, especially after GM President Harlow "Red" Curtice snookered Ford and Chryco into supporting a 1957 ban on factory backed racing he had persuaded the Automobile Manufacturers Association (AMA) to adopt. With Chevrolet's big three rivals sidelined and the back door at GM R&D still wide open to any racers who might wander past, Chevrolet drivers scored fifty-five victories in the next three seasons.

Big-block power was added to Chevrolet's racing arsenal in 1958 and a new four-speed made its debut the following year. In addition to the 305hp, 348ci/four-speed combination under the hood, Reed's "Bat Wing" Impala also rolled on one of the first sets of Goodyear racing rubber used in stock car racing. It was a winning combination.

Pole speed for the 1959 Southern 500 was 123.734mph and Reed averaged 111.836mph while winning the race. The replica of Reed's winning Impala on display at the Joe Weatherly Stock Car Museum in Darlington features the same racing livery and spartan but basically stock interior of the real car. It was restored and donated to the Museum by the Goodyear Tire and Rubber Co. to commemorate Goodyear's first major NASCAR victory.

Fireball was the master of all he surveyed from this cockpit at Daytona in 1962. Note the standard door panels, essentially stock bucket seat, and mostly unaltered dash. Roll-up window glass was still part of the package as was a taped up factory steering wheel. Still in place is the single side bar roll cage that satisfied the NASCAR rules book in 1962.

FIREBALL ROBERTS' 1962 CATALINA

Glenn "Fireball" Roberts and Henry "Smokey" Yunick were both standouts in NASCAR's early days. Fireball's aggressive driving and clean-cut good looks made him an early fan favorite. Smokey's mechanical creativity made both his "Best Damn Garage in Town" in Daytona Beach and his race cars legendary. When the two paired up for the 1962 NASCAR season, success was almost a forgone conclusion.

NASCAR Grand National stock cars circa 1962 were still fairly closely related in silhouette to their assembly line counterparts. In fact, cars like Fireball's Catalina actually started life as assembly line-built "bodies in white" that were shipped sans suspension and drivetrain to a shop like Smokey's for race preparation. Thus, they still carried hinged doors, mostly stock sheet metal, and factory bumpers. Things were far from stock under the skin, however. Reinforced suspension components, "breathed on" drivetrains, and gutted control cabins were the order of the day.

1962 CATALINA
Wheelbase: 120in
Weight: 3,835lb
Suspension: Screw jack-adjustable, reinforced "A" frames and HD coils, two shocks per wheel (front); screw jack-adjustable, HD coils, trailing arms, twin shocks per wheel, and Pontiac differential with floating hubs (rear)
Brakes: Reinforced shoes/ventilated drums
Engine: 421ci, ohv, 1-4V, V-8, 405hp
Transmission: Borg Warner, floor-shifted, four-speed manual
Speed at Darlington: 130mph

Though Yunick had had a major role in Chevrolet's first-ever GN win, he was race preparing Pontiacs in the early sixties. Unlike the "corporate" Chevrolet small-blocks that have been found under the hoods of all GM (Pontiac, Chevrolet, Buick, Oldsmobile) stockers since the late seventies, in 1962 Pontiac engineers had their own ideas about how best to make horsepower, and they molded those concepts in cast iron. The Super Duty 421 engine that powered Fireball's Catalina was clearly superior to all others on the circuit.

That fact was proved the preceding year when Super Duty powered Ponchos won thirty of the fifty-two Grand National races, including one by Marvin Panch in the 1961 Daytona 500 in a Smokey Yunick-prepared car. The Catalina that Smokey prepared for Fireball with covert factory support was both smaller and more powerful (at 405hp) than the Bonneville that Panch had driven the previous season, and that boded well for Speedweeks 1962. At Daytona, Fireball ran a hot lap of 156.999mph in qualifying, convincingly won one of the two twin 100 mile (mi) qualifying races, and outpaced Richard Petty to win the Daytona 500 itself.

Fireball and his fellow Pontiac drivers romped through their competition in 1962,

Like all GN stockers of the era, Junior Johnson's Impala appears from a distance to be quite stock. That's because most of its body panels and suspension components originated on a GM assembly line. Race preparation and the installation of an exotic, purpose-built racing drivetrain ended all resemblance with every day grocery getters, however. Notice the subtly flared fenders that cleared the racing rubber of the day but probably made modern, 18 second (sec) four-tire changes a physical impossibility.

winning twenty-two of that year's fifty-five races. Fireball accounted for three wins, including the Firecracker 250, which made him the absolute "king" of Daytona that year. Pontiac's NASCAR dominance ended with the withdrawal of factory backing the following year but not before Poncho drivers recorded an impressive two-year total of fifty-two wins in 105 events entered.

The 1962 Catalina that Fireball drove to victory in 1962 is currently on display at the International Motorsports Hall of Fame in Talladega.

JUNIOR JOHNSON'S 1963 IMPALA

Automotive rivalries are always intense, whether they are between different manufacturers or internal divisions of the same company. And that's why the folks in GM's Bow Tie division were none too happy in 1961 and 1962. The burr under their saddle was the absolute dominance enjoyed by sister division Pontiac in NASCAR racing.

That's why Chevrolet engineers started with a fresh sheet of drafting paper to design an all-new, competition-only big-block. Abandoning the inline valves and shallow combustion chambers of the earlier 348 and 409 engines, they penned an all new design featuring porcupine or poly angle valve placement and an HD, four-bolt main journaled block. Cubic inches grew to 427, and early testing suggested the new engine would spell superspeedway success in a race-ready Impala chassis.

NASCAR stars like Robert "Junior" Johnson, Rex White, and Smokey Yunick tested the "Mystery Motor" at a secret southwestern desert site. Performance was so impressive that Yunick and Johnson immediately abandoned their Pontiac machinery and, along with White, campaigned the new 427 in a Chevy chassis in 1963.

Unfortunately, GM executives were worried about the repercussions of their obvious violation of the AMA's ban on factory racing (the Mystery Motor was, after all, a race-only engine). Just before the season began, they canceled the program and recalled the forty-eight engines already produced. Johnson and the others strongly protested, so GM relented and allowed the new 427s to race—but only with the limited supply of parts already produced.

Mystery Motor drivers quickly made their mark at Daytona. Johnny Rutherford (in Smokey's Impala) and Junior Johnson easily won their respective 100mi qualifiers. Johnson ran a qualifying lap of 165.183mph (fully 8mph faster than the previous year's pole speed). Unfortunately, the new engine's lack of R & D time proved its undoing, and mechanical problems plagued it during the 500—and for the rest of the season. Though Johnson's #3 Impala often set the fast lap in qualifying, it was seldom

---

1963 IMPALA
Wheelbase: 119in
Weight: 3,877lb
Suspension: Screw jack-adjustable, reinforced "A" frames and HD coils, twin shocks per wheel (front); screw jack-adjustable, HD coils and trailing arms, twin shocks per wheel and Chevrolet differential with floating hubs (rear)
Brakes: Reinforced shoes/ventilated drums
Engine: 427ci, ohv, 1-4V, V-8, 427hp
Transmission: Borg Warner, floor-shifted, four-speed manual
Speed at Darlington: 133mph

Junior Johnson spent his 1963 race days strapped into a slightly modified Chevrolet bucket seat and just behind a basically stock dash and steering wheel. Note the frail looking roll cage assembly and uncomfortable looking steering wheel wrap.

around at the finish of the race. The scarcity of parts took a major toll, too. At season's end, the Mystery Motor drivers had scored just eight victories.

Junior Johnson's restored Mystery Motor Impala is on display at the Joe Weatherly Stock Car Museum in Darlington.

FIREBALL ROBERTS' 1963 GALAXIE

Ford racing efforts received a serious setback in 1957 when then-corporate chief Robert McNamara pulled the financial rug from beneath the racers' feet. After struggling through the next few seasons on their own, Ford teams like the fabled Holman & Moody operation were well positioned when Henry Ford II decided to return to racing in the early sixties. By 1963, the Ford/H&M juggernaut was again at full speed and had attracted many of the era's top drivers.

Fireball Roberts, arguably NASCAR's first superstar driver, accepted a factory backed Holman & Moody ride partway into the 1963 season, and soon his "Passino Purple" Galaxie (named after Ford's racing chief, Jacques Passino) led the pack.

23

1963 GALAXIE
Wheelbase: 119in
Weight: 3,715lb
Suspension: Screw jack-adjustable, reinforced
  "A" frames and HD coils, twin shocks per
  wheel (front); HD leaf spring mounted Ford
  differential with floating hubs, twin shocks
  per wheel (rear)
Brakes: Reinforced shoes/ventilated drums
Engine: 427ci, ohv, 1-4V, V-8, 410hp
Transmission: Borg Warner, floor-shifted, four-
  speed manual
Speed at Darlington: 133mph

Fireball's H&M debut came in March at Bristol, where he won the Southeastern 500. His next victory came at Daytona, his home track, in the Firecracker 400, and he won at Darlington in the Southern 500, finishing the season fourth in points.

Fireball's Galaxie used one of Ford's new 427ci big-block "FE" engines. That new-for-1963 power plant would be the basis for Ford's domination of stock car racing for most of the rest of the decade. In 1963 trim, the "Low Riser" 427 sported a single four-barrel carburetor, a high-rise aluminum intake manifold, and a pair of cast iron headers. In between was a cross bolt main journaled block and beefed-up reciprocating assembly that cranked out

Fireball Roberts' Holman & Moody prepped Galaxie was the class of any starting grid it graced. Built from a full framed "body in white" at H&M's Charlotte airport facility, the car featured a screw jack-adjustable, "A" frame front suspension and a leaf spring mounted corporate 9in differential. The chassis rolled on H&M's reinforced steel rims and narrow (by modern standards) 7 1/4in wide Goodyear racing rubber. *Mike Slade*

more than the 410hp advertised on the #22 car's hood.

Fireball "re-upped" with Ford and Holman & Moody for 1964 and was slated to start a new career as a personal representative for a major brewing company–a first for an athlete in any American sport. Tragically, a horrendous crash precipitated by Ned Jarrett and Junior Johnson early in the Memorial Day running of the World 600 cut Fireball's life much too short.

This replica of Fireball's Galaxie was constructed from a 1964 Holman & Moody Galaxie following his death. It is on display at the Joe Weatherly Stock Car Museum in Darlington.

TINY LUND'S 1964 GALAXIE

Dwayne "Tiny" Lund became a national hero in 1963 when he rescued Marvin Panch from an overturned, burning race car just prior to the running of the Daytona 500. When nominated by the injured Panch to fill his Wood Brothers Ford's seat during the 500, Lund drove to a storybook win that would have been as hard to believe as the plot of "Days of Thunder" had it not actually happened. Unfortunately, Tiny's success did not translate into a full factory ride that season, and he continued to compete as a journeyman independent at selected races.

Late in 1964 Lund began to campaign this 427 Galaxie. It was built over a stock factory frame that was reinforced to sustain the rigors of racing. Modifications included cutting and rewelding the front control arms for both rigidity and revised steering geometry. Twin hydraulic shocks were added to each wheel, and they mounted to tubular towers that were added to the frame. Screw jack spring perches were added atop each front coil to permit pit stop adjustment of the car's handling characteristics.

The Galaxie's rear suspension consisted of non-adjustable leaf springs tailored to the needs of each particular track via the use of extra leaves, unequal height lowering blocks, and multi-position rear shackles. Twin shocks were again used to control jounce, and a modified Eaton power steering pump circulated differential lube to and from a remote cooler.

Unlike the "bucks up" teams on the circuit, Tiny did not have access to the latest iteration of the Ford 427 racing engine (which for 1964 featured radically raised ports that spawned the "High Riser" nickname). So he soldiered on with the previous year's technology. His engine cranked out well over 410hp, but that was not enough to catch cars like Richard Petty's Hemi-powered Plymouth or Fred Lorenzen's HR-motorvated Galaxie.

Even though Tiny's Galaxie didn't win fame through victories, it achieved a fair amount of notoriety as the "camera" car for an early attempt to document NASCAR

1964 GALAXIE
Wheelbase: 119in
Weight: 3,672lb
Suspension: Screw jack-adjustable, reinforced "A" frames and HD coils, twin shocks per wheel (front); HD leaf spring-mounted Ford differential with floating hubs, twin shocks per wheel (rear)
Brakes: Reinforced shoes/ventilated drums
Engine: 427ci, ohv, 1-4V, V-8, 410hp
Transmission: Borg Warner, floor-shifted, four-speed manual
Speed at Darlington: 133mph

1964 Galaxies were LARGE cars from any angle. Imagine a NASCAR field made up of forty or so similarly sized pachyderms and you can well understand the oft-used racing expression "rubbing fenders." The 1964-vintage Grand National cars still sported full factory glass and all manner of assembly line brightwork.

Left
Though not a top of the line High Riser motor, the 427 in Tiny's Galaxie was still potent enough to propel it around tracks like Daytona at triple-digit velocities. And that's no small achievement for a car carrying enough sheet metal to make three Toyotas.

racing by west coast cinematographer, Dick Wallen.

Ohio enthusiast Bob Berlin restored and owns Lund's 1964 GN stocker.

FRED LORENZEN'S 1965 HOLMAN & MOODY GALAXIE

Though "good ol' boy" NASCAR stock car racing is strongly associated with the southern United States, one of the sport's most beloved heroes, Fred Lorenzen, was born far north of the Mason/ Dixon line. Lorenzen first came south in 1960 as an independent driver but met with little success. Luckily, his natural driving talents caught the eye of Ralph Moody (half of Ford's Holman & Moody racing factory), and "Fearless Freddy" was soon behind the wheel of a factory backed, H&M-prepared Galaxie.

In 1963, Lorenzen was the first driver to pocket more than $100,000 in a single season when he won six races and had twenty-one top five finishes. Lorenzen scored the biggest win of his career in 1965 in the rain-shortened Daytona 500 in a trademark

Ford's slab-sided '65 Galaxie looks about as slick as a brick aerodynamically. But, of course, that didn't really matter when you had a high-revving, 427ci big-block under the hood with which to punch holes in the air. Stock window glass and door handles remained in place in 1965, but chrome side trim had mostly disappeared.

white and blue, #28 Holman & Moody Ford. He also had a particularly good year at Charlotte in 1965, winning both the grueling World 600 and the National 500.

Beyond its race success, Lorenzen's H&M '65 has other significance. Specifically, 1965 was the year Holman & Moody perfected the rear steer suspension components still found under many nineties Winston Cup stock cars–regardless of their manufacturer.

Though it may be hard for GM enthusiasts to accept, most of the Chevrolet (and Olds, Buick, and Pontiac) victories scored in the modern era were by cars rolling on essentially the same underpinnings as Lorenzen's '65 Ford Galaxie. In fact, reinforced Galaxie lower control arms, Galaxie steering boxes, screw jack-adjustable Galaxie coil springs, Galaxie drag links, tie rods and even Galaxie-based 9in Ford differentials can all still be found in 1990s Winston Cup cars.

One component on Lorenzen's car not found under the hood of a modern stock car is the massive, big-block motor; engines like that 427ci Medium Riser engine have been absent from GN/WC competition since the early seventies.

One of the cars that Lorenzen campaigned in 1965 has been restored by Gastonia, North Carolina's Kim Haynes.

SMOKEY YUNICK'S 1966 CHEVELLE

GM's 1963 decision to terminate all factory support (even the covert kind) for motorsports competition left Chevrolet racers high and dry. Most began racing Fomoco or Mopar products. Henry "Smokey" Yunick has always had the habit of going his own way, so, it comes as no surprise to learn Smokey campaigned Bow Tie race cars long after the factory had officially abandoned racing.

In the mid-sixties Smokey built a series of 1966 Chevelles that have transcended the racing record to enter the lofty realm of legend. One of the cars was built to run Daytona in 1967 and has come to be known as the 3/4 scale Chevelle. Hard-charging Curtis "Pops" Turner (a nickname earned because of his fondness for popping competitors right off the track) put that car in the 500 with a record qualifying speed of 180.831mph–fully 5mph better than the fastest 1966 qualifier. Disgruntled competitors protested the car's allegedly scaled-down silhouette, so NASCAR officials and Smokey used one of the first body templates to compare its shape to an assembly line version.

If the Chevelle that Smokey built for the 1967 season bent the rules book a bit, then the '66 that he prepared for 1968 threw the bloody thing clear out the window. The car shown here represented the sum total of all that Smokey had learned about both going fast and liberally interpreting NASCAR's

---

1965 HOLMAN & MOODY GALAXIE
Wheelbase: 119in
Weight: 4,000lb
Suspension: Screw jack-adjustable, reinforced "A" frames and HD coils, twin shocks per wheel (front); screw jack-adjustable HD coils and trailing arms, Ford 9in differential with floating hubs, twin shocks per wheel (rear)
Brakes: Reinforced shoes/ventilated drums
Engine: 427ci, ohv, 1-4V, V-8, 425hp
Transmission: Ford T&C, floor-shifted, four-speed manual
Speed at Darlington: 137mph

Smokey's Chevelle incorporated many subtle tricks to improve its aerodynamics—only some of which were permitted. Take a close look at the car's front bumper. If it looks a tad wide, it should. That's because Smokey had it widened by a full 2in to create a rudimentary spoiler. Other innovations included a full belly pan, offset front and rear frame snouts (designed to move the car's center of gravity), fully adjustable, fabricated control arms, and a vortex generator recessed into the roofline. NASCAR inspectors determined that Smokey had been too creative by half and banned the car from competition.

1966 CHEVELLE
Wheelbase: 115-118in
Weight: 3,800lb
Suspension: Screw jack-adjustable, fabricated
    control arms and HD coils, twin shocks per
    wheel (front); screw jack-adjustable D coils
    and trailing arms, Ford 9in differential with
    floating hubs, twin shocks per wheel (rear)
Brakes: Reinforced shoes/ventilated drums
Engine: 410ci, ohv, 1-4V, V-8, 425hp
Transmission: Borg Warner, floor-shifted, four-
    speed manual
Speed at Darlington: 140mph

rules. Though at a glance the car appeared to be stock, in fact, Smokey had "cheated" the car up beyond belief.

Take, for example, the sectioned and widened (by about 2in) front bumper that served as an air foil. Then there was the off-set frame that placed the engine much farther to the left than was legal, for better handling. Or, how about the completely fabricated frame that incorporated an aerodynamically slick, flush belly pan which kept chassis protuberances out of the flow of air? And don't forget the subtle depression in the roof line—a vortex generator to enhance the function of the minuscule 2in rear deck spoiler the rules permitted. Unfortunately, this Chevelle never made it through the inspection process, and in a fit of pique, Smokey drove the car from the track across town to his Beach Street shop. The local newspapers the next day claimed the jaunt was made without the benefit of a fuel tank. Voila, another NASCAR legend was created.

Smokey's Chevelle never turned a competitive lap. After languishing in a Georgia salvage yard for several years, Smokey retrieved the car and restored it to its 1968 trim. Floyd Garrett is the car's current owner and plans to display the Chevelle at his Pigeon Forge, Tennessee, museum.

FRED LORENZEN'S 1967 H&M FAIRLANE

Ford racers campaigned dirigible class Galaxie stock cars until the 1966 season. The continuing controversy over the legality of Ford's 427 overhead camshaft (ohc) Hemi led Henry Ford II to pull the plug on Fomoco's racing effort at the beginning of that season in much the same way

During the mid-sixties, Smokey Yunick built a series of Chevelles for drivers like Curtis Turner, Gordon Johncock, and Mario Andretti. Each carried Smokey's trademark black and gold racing livery and the "lucky" number 13. Smokey firmly believed that if the NASCAR rules book didn't specifically prohibit a particular modification, then it must be legal. As a result, his Chevelles bent the rules book to the breaking point and became a part of NASCAR mythology.

that Chryco had opted to boycott in 1965, when its Hemi was outlawed.

While most Ford drivers cooled their heels, the always innovative Bud Moore opted to campaign a downsized Mercury Comet in an attempt to keep up with the "re-legalized" Hemi cars that were back on the circuit. In the process, Moore proved the viability of mid-sized Ford race cars. When the boycotting Ford teams returned late in

the season, they, too, fielded intermediates.

Among them was the 427 Tunnel Port-powered Fairlane that Fearless Freddy Lorenzen drove during his last season with Holman & Moody. Unlike earlier H&M Galaxies, his '67 Fairlane was built around a unit body rather than full frame chassis. To make that work, Ralph Moody developed a semi-fabricated snout based on frame components from the '65 Galaxie line. Once fitted with '65 Galaxie style suspension members, the whole affair was grafted onto the rear two-thirds of the stock Fairlane unit body to create what came to be called a half-chassis car. Rear suspension components consisted of heavy duty leaf springs and a Ford 9in differential.

In an attempt to appease Ford corporate officials, NASCAR permitted Ford racers to run unhomologated Tunnel Port-headed 427 engines and dual four-barrel carburetors, even though those engines were never available in a road-going Ford. The gaping ports of the Tunnel Port "FE" heads, coupled with eight barrels of carburetion, produced unexcelled breathing and truckloads of horsepower. Factory literature for street-going 427s claimed 425hp; it's likely that a NASCAR-spec Tunnel Port churned out substantially closer to 500.

By 1966, Ford's Galaxie had grown to nearly block-long size. The advent of downsized, "half chassis" Fairlane race cars late in that season put Blue Oval racers on a more even footing with their Chryco rivals, who had campaigned intermediates since the early sixties. Relatively stock sheet metal and exterior trim were still mandated by the 1967 rules book. Roll-up safety glass windows were still used on superspeedways but no longer were mandatory (their absence on this particular chassis mark it as a short track car).

As in preceding years, Lorenzen's control cabin was based primarily on production components. Still in place, too, was the lanyard-operated trap door and strobe light assembly that permitted "in flight" inspection of the all important right front tire.

Lorenzen auspiciously introduced his downsized '67 stocker by winning one of the 100mi Daytona 500 qualifiers, and in the race he ran second to Mario Andretti, who drove an identically prepared H&M Fairlane. Unfortunately for his fans, Lorenzen did not capitalize on that promising

1967 H&M FAIRLANE
Wheelbase: 115-118in
Weight: 3,500lb (minimum)
Suspension: Screw jack-adjustable, reinforced
   control arms ('65 Galaxie) and HD coils, twin
   shocks per wheel (front); HD leaf springs,
   Ford 9in differential with floating hubs, twin
   shocks per wheel rear)
Brakes: Reinforced H&M shoes/ventilated drums
Engine: 427ci, ohv, 1 or 2-4V, V-8, 550-600hp
Transmission: Ford T&C, floor-shifted, four-
   speed manual
Speed at Darlington: 148mph

start and, in fact, retired later in the year.

One of the Fairlanes he drove that year is on display at either the International Motorsports Hall of Fame in Talladega, or the Joe Weatherly Stock Car Museum in Darlington.

RICHARD PETTY'S 1967 PLYMOUTH

1967 was the year that the motorsports media crowned Richard Petty the "King" of stock car racing, and it's easy to understand why. At season's end, King Richard had won an incredible twenty-seven of the forty-eight races he started, and had top five finishes in eleven more. Ten wins came consecutively during a two-month period when Petty reserved victory lane exclusively for his electric blue Plymouth.

Based on a unit construction, Satellite intermediate body, Petty's car represents the unique way that Chryco went racing in the sixties. Instead of employing the captured coil springs and "A" frames found under the competition, for example, Mopar racers relied on torsion bars to keep the beaks of their stockers just above the track surface. A conventional leaf sprung rear suspension was used aft but those springs supported a corporate 8 3/4in differential rather than a Ford 9in unit used by Chevrolet and Fomoco racers.

And instead of the wedge-headed engines used by most other GN stockers, Mopar drivers' cars were powered by a Hemi-headed version of the 426ci big-block engine.

Of the forty-eight races contested in 1967, Petty and his fellow Hemi drivers won thirty-four times. In winning the Grand National championship, King Richard

At first glance, the boxy Satellite that Richard Petty drove in 1967 doesn't look to be a likely candidate for superspeedway success. Slab sides, a nearly perpendicular front profile, and a generally boxy silhouette seemingly run counter to the needs of high-speed aerodynamics. Of course, when there's a 600hp, 426 Hemi engine under the hood, the puny forces of nature pale in comparison. Or, at least, that's what seemed to happen in 1967 when "King" Richard Petty used the "elephant" motor in his electric blue race car to bludgeon the competition. *Mike Slade*

1967 PLYMOUTH
Wheelbase: 115in
Weight: 3,500lb (minimum)
Suspension: Adjustable torsion bars, reinforced "A" frames, twin shocks per wheel (front); HD leaf springs, Chryco differential with floating hubs, twin shocks per wheel (rear)
Brakes: Reinforced shoes/ventilated drums
Engine: 426ci, hemispherically chambered, ohv, 1-4V, V-8, 550-600hp
Transmission: Chrysler 833, floor-shifted, four-speed manual
Speed at Darlington: 143.423mph

Fomoco's 1968 introduction of radically fastbacked Ford and Mercury intermediates was the first salvo in the aerodynamic wars that Fomoco and Chryco waged the following two seasons. Though powered by the same 427 Tunnel Port engines used the previous season, the car's aerodynamic profile helped the car run nearly 10mph faster at Daytona than '67 Fairlanes had the year before. That performance helped the NASCAR community finally realize the real secret to speed was not just increasing horsepower and cubic inches every racing season. Wind tunnel time has since become just as important as dyno engine development on the circuit.

scored two superspeedway wins at Darlington. His mastery of Darlington's "Lady-in-Black" included a pole-winning lap of 143.423mph, leading 342 of the Southern 500's 364 laps, setting a new record average speed of 103.423mph for the 500 miles, and finishing more than five laps ahead of runner-up David Pearson. Yet it was on the short tracks that year that his Hemi's torque permitted him to totally master the competition.

One of the cars that Petty drove to his "coronation" is on display at the Joe Weatherly Stock Car Museum in Darlington.

LeeRoy Yarbrough's 1968 Mercury Cyclone

Ford and Mercury racers had given up much to their Mopar counterparts during most of the sixties. While forced to campaign full-sized Galaxies and Marauders due to factory politics, Mopar drivers like Richard Petty had driven lighter and more nimble intermediates almost since the dawn of the decade. Chrysler's introduction of the 426 Hemi engine in 1964 and ultimate homologation of that motor in 1966 had put Blue Oval drivers at an even greater disadvantage. Henry Ford II's failure to win sanctioning body approval for the 427 single overhead cam and the boxiness of both Ford full-sized and intermediate cars made 1966 and 1967 fairly frustrating years for Ford and Mercury fans.

That all changed in 1968 when both Ford and Mercury introduced radically redesigned Fairlane and Montego lines that featured exaggerated, nearly flat rear roof lines.

Jacksonville, Florida, driver LeeRoy Yarbrough was one of Ford's factory backed drivers in 1968, piloting Junior Johnson's (who by then had hung up his driving gloves) factory backed Mercury Cyclone. For the next two seasons that duo experienced unprecedented success on NASCAR's high banks. Though forced to campaign the 427 Tunnel Port engine, the clean, windswept lines of Yarbrough's Mercury helped close the gap with the Mopar cars from the first race of the season. Yarbrough's #26 Cyclone (Johnson would change the car's number to #98 late in the season to improve the team's luck!) finished a close second to fellow Mercury driver Cale Yarborough's Wood Brothers-prepared car in the Daytona 500, then reprised that role in the Atlanta 500 and at Daytona in July in the Firecracker 400. LeeRoy's then-#98 Cyclone won its first superspeedway race of the season at the Dixie 500 at Atlanta. He netted $87,919, third-highest in purse money that season.

When Yarbrough's race cars got more aerodynamic Spoiler II/Talladega noses in 1969, he won the Daytona 500, the Rebel 400, the World 600, the Firecracker 400, the Dixie 500, the Southern 500, and the American 500. Unfortunately, 1969 was the high water mark of Yarbrough's career. A serious

Power for LeeRoy's Cyclone was provided by Tunnel Port-headed 427 Ford engines similar to the "FE" big-block in this replica. Performance was impressive but still somewhat lacking compared to Chrysler's Hemi. Fortunately, the car's aerodynamic advantage more than evened the score. With the addition of aerodynamic beaks and Boss 429 Hemi engines, the same basic race cars became the kings of the Superspeedway.

1968 MERCURY CYCLONE
Wheelbase: 115-118in
Weight: 3,900lb (minimum)
Suspension: Screw jack-adjustable, reinforced control arms ('65 Galaxie) and HD coils, twin shocks per wheel (front); HD, screw jack-adjustable leaf springs, Ford 9in differential with floating hubs, twin shocks per wheel (rear)
Brakes: Reinforced H&M shoes/ventilated drums
Engine: 427ci, ohv, 1 or 2-4V, V-8, 550-600hp
Transmission: Ford T&C, floor-shifted, four-speed manual
Speed at Darlington: 144mph

shunt at Indy and subsequent illness brought his driving days to a premature conclusion. This replica of his early 1968 Junior Johnson-prepared Cyclone is privately owned by Davidson, North Carolina's Alex Beam.

A. J. Foyt's 1969 Ford Torino

Anthony Joseph Foyt, Jr., has been called by many the greatest racing driver of all time. He has excelled in just about every form of motorsports he has tried, including NASCAR Grand National stock car racing.

Though never a regular on the circuit, Foyt did stray south from his usual USAC haunts long enough and regularly enough to score several major GN victories, including the 1965 Firecracker 400, the 1970 Motor Trend 500 (at Riverside), the 1971 and 1972 Miller High Life 500s (at Ontario), the 1971 Atlanta 500, and, most notably, the 1972 Daytona 500.

In 1969, Foyt was part of Ford's "Going Thing" and fielded a Jack Bowsher Torino at selected NASCAR events. Based on the swoopy fastback intermediates introduced in 1968, Foyt's Torino featured an exagger-

A. J. Foyt's greatest fame, of course, has come in open wheel competition. Even so, he was no stranger to NASCAR racing in the sixties and seventies. In 1969 he drove slippery Torino Cobras ("short" nosed cars) and even sleeker Torino Talladegas (the Cobra's "long" nosed successor) for Jack Bowsher in selected NASCAR events.

The great success enjoyed by "short" nosed Ford and Mercury intermediates in 1968 and early 1969 can be directly attributed to the dramatically swooping rear roof line the cars shared. By 1968 it had become clear to manufacturers and racers alike that aerodynamic performance was every bit as important as horsepower.

ated fastback roofline that swept from the "A" pillar to the tip of the deck lid in a nearly unbroken arc.

At Foyt's first outing in the Bowsher '69, at Riverside in February of 1969, his Torino was outfitted with the same "stock" front clip as the car pictured here since Ford's debut of the new Talladega line was slated for Daytona. The 427 Tunnel Port engine was used, but for 1969 it came with a single Holley Dominator induction system instead of the 8V set up used previously. Foyt used his UASC left/right experience to win the pole with a hot lap of 110.323mph. He led the first twenty-seven laps but finished second to the Torino of Richard Petty, who, in storybook fashion, won his very first outing in a Ford.

At Daytona, Foyt finished fourth, then was absent from the circuit until the National 500 at Charlotte in October. Unfortunately, that was turned into an unhappy homecoming on lap eighty-eight when the Boss 429 engine (unveiled in March in Atlanta) lost its structural integrity.

The car pictured here is thought to be one of Foyt's '69 mounts due to the letters

1969 FORD TORINO
Wheelbase: 115-118in
Weight: 3,900lb (minimum)
Suspension: Screw jack-adjustable, reinforced control arms ('65 Galaxie) and HD coils, twin shocks per wheel (front); HD, screw jack-adjustable leaf springs, Ford 9in differential with floating hubs, twin shocks per wheel (rear)
Brakes: Reinforced H&M shoes/ventilated drums
Engine: 427ci, ohv, 1-4V, V-8, 550-600hp
Transmission: Ford T&C, floor-shifted, four-speed manual
Speed at Darlington: 151mph

"A.J." found inside one of its door panels during restoration. It belongs to Davidson, North Carolina's Alex Beam.

DONNIE ALLISON'S 1969 TORINO TALLADEGA

The "aero wars" waged by Fomoco and Chryco were the culmination and concluding chapter of the factory backed racing competition that had resumed nearly ten years earlier with the abandonment of the AMA racing ban. Fomoco fired the first shot in 1968 with the introduction of sleek new Ford and Mercury intermediates. Chrysler, dismayed by those cars' immediate super-

Talladegas, like all Ford intermediates of the sixties, rolled on "half chassis" underpinnings. After beginning life as assembly line unit bodies, their front shock towers were torched off and replaced with a fabricated snout and suspension based on '65 H&M GN Galaxie components. A "Big T's" rear suspension wasn't all that far removed from assembly line trim.

40

Though Torino Talladegas lack the radical contours of their Mopar winged car competition, the record book marks them as the ultimate aero warriors during the 1969 and 1970 NASCAR seasons. Basically stock (in NASCAR terms) Torinos from the "A" pillars rearward, Talladegas featured a front clip that had been lengthened 5in and then narrowed with an eye toward more efficiently scything through the air. The design, arrived at by Ralph Moody and Fomoco engineers, was both simple and effective.

speedway domination, quickly tried to mend the Charger's aerodynamic woes by making that car's grille and backlight flush with surrounding body work. That new aero-variant built specifically for NASCAR racing made its debut at Daytona in February 1969.

Side glass was no longer used on short track cars in 1969 and was mandated out of existence all together in 1970. When this happened, builders bulged their race car's side cage bars into the now hollow door skin creating more crush room and driver safety. Four driver's side bars and multiple rear diagonals were standard parts of a NASCAR chassis in 1969.

1969 TORINO TALLADEGA

Wheelbase: 115-118in

Weight: 3,900lb (minimum)

Suspension: Screw jack-adjustable, reinforced control arms ('65 Galaxie or fully fabricated) and HD coils, twin shocks per wheel (front); HD screw jack-adjustable leaf springs, Ford 9in differential with floating hubs, twin shocks per wheel (rear)

Brakes: Reinforced H&M shoes/ventilated drums

Engine: Either 427ci, ohv, 1-4V, V-8 (Tunnel Port/wedge head), 550-600hp or 429ci, ohv, 1-4V, V-8 (Boss 429/hemi head) wet sump lubrication, 600-650hp

Transmission: Ford T&C, floor-shifted, four-speed manual

Speed at Darlington: 151mph

Unfortunately for the "Dodge Boys," Ford engineers and Ralph Moody had been busy during the off-season, and they too had a specially prepared and homologated aero-warrior ready to do battle. The car was basically a rebaked version of the previous year's all-conquering Torino, with an extended, drooped snout and flush-fitting grille. Ford racing execs dubbed the car the Torino Talladega after Bill France's new 2.66mi superspeedway in Alabama.

First blood for the "Big T" came at the '69 Daytona 500. Fomoco aero warriors went on to win the '69 and '70 factory backed aerodynamic wars. All told, Talladegas won twenty-nine of the 102 GN races contested during those seasons, more than any other body style. 1967 NASCAR Rookie of the Year Donnie Allison drove a poppy red #27 to three of those victories: the '69 National 500, the '70 Firecracker 400, and the '70 World 600.

A replica of the Talladegas driven to those victories is fittingly on display at the International Motorsports Hall of Fame, trackside in Talladega.

RICHARD PETTY'S 1969 TORINO TALLADEGA

Chrysler's "Dodge Boys" had been shocked to find that their new for 1968 "fuselage bodied" Charger line was no match for Fomoco's equally new Fairlanes and Montegos—even though the Chryco cars enjoyed a horsepower advantage. The obvious impediment to their performance had to be aerodynamics. And, in fact, the sleek looking Chargers came equipped with a cavernous, air-grabbing grille opening and a lift-inducing tunneled backlight. A hasty "redo" of the design for racing purposes resulted in the Charger 500. Chryco pinned its corporate hopes on that new design and left the Plymouth line untouched.

It wasn't enough—either to win or to keep Plymouth superstar Richard Petty in the fold. When the NASCAR tour opened

Petty began 1969 under the power of the same 427 Tunnel Port engines he had competed against in his Plymouths since 1967. Later in the year, Petty once again had a Hemi at his command—a "Blue Crescent" Boss 429 Ford Hemi, that is.

1969 TORINO TALLADEGA
Wheelbase: 115-118in
Weight: 3,900lb (minimum)
Suspension: Screw jack-adjustable, reinforced
    control arms ('65 Galaxie or fully fabricated)
    and HD coils, twin shocks per wheel (front);
    HD screw jack-adjustable leaf springs, Ford
    9in differential with floating hubs, twin shocks
    per wheel (rear)
Brakes: Reinforced H&M shoes/ventilated drums
Engine: Either 427ci, ohv, 1-4V, V-8 (Tunnel
    Port/wedge head), 550-600hp; or 429ci, ohv,
    1-4V, V-8 Boss 429/hemi head), wet sump
    lubrication, 600-650hp
Transmission: Ford T&C, floor-shifted, four-
    speed manual
Speed at Darlington: 151mph

Though it might come as a shock to some, Richard Petty did campaign a #43 Talladega very much like this one during the 1969 GN season. Although possessing absolutely no Ford experience at the time, Petty and his crew were able to score nine wins in their Fords that year and finish the season fewer than 300 points behind fellow Talladega driver David Pearson in the driving championship.

the season at Riverside, King Richard was there with an electric blue Ford Torino Cobra. Though his Mopar fans mourned Ford's coup, Petty seemed little perturbed by the switch. He promptly won his first road race ever in that car, and recorded eight more wins and thirty-one top five finishes in a Ford. By the end of his first (and, as it turned out, only) season with the "Blue Oval," Petty was second to H&M Talladega driver David Pearson in the championship points race and $129,906 richer. In addition to his win at Riverside, he also won at Martinsville and Dover.

The Petty blue Talladega pictured here was restored by Davidson, North Carolina's Alex Beam and is currently on display in the Petty Museum in Level Cross, North Carolina.

BOBBY ISAAC'S 1969 DODGE CHARGER DAYTONA

Though Dodge's new-for-1968 "fuselage bodied" Charger line looked streamlined and sleek while at rest, it actually was a fairly dirty design aerodynamically—at least at speeds beyond the 160mph it took to be competitive on the NASCAR high banks that year.

So Bob Roger and the engineers in Chrysler's performance division went back to the drawing board and ultimately produced arguably the most radical American automobile to ever roll down an assembly line or a pit road, the Dodge Charger Daytona. Based on the failed Charger 500 package, the Daytonas that rolled out in the middle of the 1969 season featured a pointy sheet metal snout that literally sliced the air in two while keeping the car's front tires

The secret to Petty's Ford success (and that of other Talladega drivers in 1969) was the extended snout that had been grafted onto their Torino Cobras' noses. Though subtle in appearance, especially in comparison to Dodge's "winged" cars, Ford's Talladega was actually the true NASCAR King in 1969 and 1970. Talladegas and Spoiler IIs (their Mercury cousins) won twenty-three of thirty-six races held on tracks of 1mi or more in length those two seasons; Mopar winged cars, on the other hand, only scored thirteen "mile or more" victories.

glued to the pavement. It developed in excess of 100 positive pounds of downforce at triple-digit velocities. A soaring rear wing of twin vertical air foils and an adjustable inverted wing section served the same purpose at the rear of the car and produced enough downforce to shred racing tires if too much angle was dialed in. Between the two new extremes the car remained pretty much the same as the Charger 500s that preceded it. Hemi power was also part of the racing program.

The new Daytonas made their debut at Talladega in September of 1969. Chargin' Charlie Glotzbach ran a hot qualifying lap

Graced with a needle nosed beak and soaring rear airfoil, Bobby Isaac's '69 1/2 Dodge Daytona certainly qualifies as the wildest looking American car ever built. Its performance on the track was equally as wild.

Winged cars like his were so fast, in fact, that the treaded racing tires of the day could not hold up to the strain. As a result, the very first of the now commonplace NASCAR racing slicks were developed during the 1969 season.

of 199.466mph, and Bobby Isaac proved that near-double-ton velocity was no fluke when he earned the pole in his #71 K&K-sponsored Daytona with a speed of 196.386mph around the new 3.66mi track.

The new winged cars also put new pressures on the treaded race tires still in use at the time. Concerned about the durability of the new track surface and the endurance of their racing rubber, members of the new

Professional Drivers' Association boycotted the race. Different rubber formulas were tried and Goodyear even molded up the first treadless stock car tire but nothing seemed to work.

The race ran as scheduled (with substitute drivers in "Baby Grand" series Mustangs, Camaros, and Javelins), and journeyman driver Richard Brickhouse drove Glotzbach's Daytona to victory in a race

Perhaps the most effective part of the Daytona aero package was the lofty rear deck spoiler. Made up of twin vertical air foil supports and an adjustable center wing section, it was capable of producing more than 500lb of downforce at racing velocities.

that included a series of mandatory yellow caution periods to allow the field to change tires. The Dodge Daytona's first "real" superspeedway win didn't come until the last race of the season, when Bobby Isaac finished two full laps ahead of Donnie Allison's Torino Talladega in the Texas 500.

The Plymouth division got up to speed the following year with a radically winged and beaked stock car of its own (the Superbird), and Mopar winged car drivers won with regularity. All told, winged car drivers won most of the forty-eight races held in the 1970 season, and Bobby Isaac was crowned Grand National driving champion.

And then, it was all over. Worried about ever-increasing speeds and safety, NASCAR officials introduced the carburetor restrictor plate in 1970. When that didn't work to their satisfaction, all special body aero-cars were limited to a maximum engine size of 305ci for 1971. After just two short years, Fomoco and Chryco's aero warriors had been legislated out of existence.

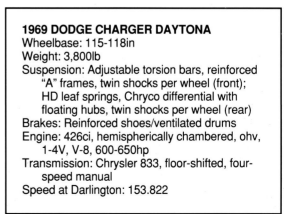

1969 DODGE CHARGER DAYTONA
Wheelbase: 115-118in
Weight: 3,800lb
Suspension: Adjustable torsion bars, reinforced "A" frames, twin shocks per wheel (front); HD leaf springs, Chryco differential with floating hubs, twin shocks per wheel (rear)
Brakes: Reinforced shoes/ventilated drums
Engine: 426ci, hemispherically chambered, ohv, 1-4V, V-8, 600-650hp
Transmission: Chrysler 833, floor-shifted, four-speed manual
Speed at Darlington: 153.822

Power for the near-200mph speeds that Daytona drivers turned in at Talladega came from a race-tuned 426 Hemi-headed big-block engine that made more than 600hp. Note the ram box intake that was used for superspeedway duty. The small fiberglass air box connected the Holley carburetor directly to the low pressure area at the base of the hood to take advantage of the ram induction effect there. The result: even more horsepower.

One of the hemi-powered Daytonas that Bobby Isaac drove in 1969 and 1970 is currently on display at the International Motorsports Hall of Fame trackside in Talladega.

BUDDY BAKER'S 1969½ DODGE DAYTONA

Speed has always been or, at least always was before the advent of the restrictor plate, the ultimate goal of NASCAR racers. After all, prize money isn't often awarded to those who finish a race in the longest time possible, is it? Lap times at Grand National events all across the country got progressively faster with each race following the premier event at Charlotte Speedway in 1949.

By the late sixties, speeds at Daytona, then the fastest track on the circuit, were nipping at the double ton mark, and it seemed just a matter of time before some fearless driver punched his stock car through the 200mph barrier. It happened in March of 1970 at Talladega when Buddy Baker blistered the tarmac of that 2.66mi long track with a 200.447mph lap during tire testing. Though unofficial, Baker's performance in the car pictured on these pages was widely touted as the first time a stock car had cracked the double ton. There was talk at the time that Bobby Allison had done so earlier in his own Hemi-powered Dodge Daytona, but, "officially," Baker's blue #88 winged car has been honored as the first past 200.

Interestingly, due to the intervention of restrictor plates and the rules-mandated extinction of big-block engines in the early

1969½ DODGE DAYTONA
Wheelbase: 115-118in
Weight: 3,800lb
Suspension: Adjustable torsion bars, reinforced "A" frames, twin shocks per wheel (front); HD leaf springs, Chryco differential with floating hubs, twin shocks per wheel (rear)
Brakes: Reinforced shoes/ventilated drums
Engine: 426ci, hemispherically chambered, ohv, 1-4V, V-8, 600-650hp
Transmission: Chrysler 833, floor-shifted, four-speed manual
Speed at Darlington: 153.822mph

Baker's blue Daytona was a formidable race car in 1969 and could probably still sit on the pole at Daytona or Talladega today. Its radically pointed, sheet metal nose cone and soaring rear deck spoiler worked exceedingly well at producing road holding downforce.

seventies, it wasn't until Cale Yarborough ran a lap of 200.503 during the 1983 Daytona 500 qualifying (immediately after which he crashed heavily) that the 200mph mark was officially reached on the NASCAR circuit.

Baker's tire test car, like his regular Cotton Owens, Day-Glo #6 Daytona at the time, was powered by a fire-breathing, 426ci version of the Chrysler Hemi. In race tune, that engine was capable of cranking out 600-650hp.

Baker's tire test car is currently on display at the International Motorsports Hall of Fame in Talladega, just outside the track where it first ran the double ton.

RICHARD PETTY'S/RAMO STOTT'S 1970 SUPERBIRDS

Plymouth racers were left out of the picture when the factory backed aero-wars erupted in 1969. While their Dodge counterparts received successively swoopier versions of the basic Charger race car, longtime Mayflower division drivers like Richard Petty were left to campaign their boxy Belvederes (or, like Petty, they left the Plymouth ranks altogether).

Things were different for Plymouth in 1970, probably because of Petty's 1969 decision to jump ship and field a Ford Talladega. Plymouth execs knew it would take an all-

Like their Dodge Daytona counterparts, Plymouth Superbirds were graced with a pointy snout and soaring rear deck wing that were designed to keep the car planted firmly on the racing surface. They looked wild, but they worked. For instance, Richard Petty's Superbird teammate, Pete Hamilton, won the Daytona 500 and both superspeedway events at Talladega in his Petty blue, #40 Superbird in 1970. King Richard's car is shown here.

new Plymouth aero-variant (and lots of money!) to get him back. They did so with the Plymouth Superbird, which amounted to a Belvedere body with a high-speed nose and rear deck airfoil. As the ads read in 1970, it was the car that got Petty back.

King Richard, his Petty Engineering teammate Dan Gurney, and Roger Mc-Clusky announced the Superbird's arrival by all finishing in the top five at the 1970 season opener at Riverside. Petty won eighteen races that season, most of them on the circuit's numerous bullring short tracks.

The winged cars were powered by race-spec versions of Chrysler's 426ci hemi-headed engine.

1970 SUPERBIRDS
Wheelbase: 115-118in
Weight: 3,800lb
Suspension: Adjustable torsion bars, reinforced "A" frames, twin shocks per wheel (front); HD leaf springs, Chryco differential with floating hubs, twin shocks per wheel (rear)
Brakes: Reinforced shoes/ventilated drums
Engine: 426ci, hemispherically chambered, ohv, 1-4V, V-8, 600-650hp
Transmission: Chrysler 833, floor-shifted, four-speed
Speed at Darlington: 153mph

One of Richard Petty's 1970 Superbirds is currently on display at his shop and museum in Level Cross, North Carolina, and

Though Petty and Hamilton got the most attention in their matched pair of electric blue Superbirds, other drivers, such as Ramo Stott, also fielded winged Plymouths. Stott campaigned his Superbird on both the ARCA and NASCAR circuits in 1970, scoring top five finishes in both.

Ramo Stott's "as raced" winged Plymouth was photographed at the International Motorsports Hall of Fame in Talladega.

DAVID PEARSON'S 1971 MERCURY CYCLONE

1972 was a turning point for racers on the NASCAR circuit. For most of the sixties, Fomoco and Chryco teams had received full funding for their race efforts directly from the factory. But factory support had all but dried up by 1971. Ford had effectively packed up its tent and gone home at the close of the 1969 season, and in 1971, even Chryco staunched its flow of factory dollars.

Long-time teams on the circuit suddenly had to scramble for sponsorship dollars, and some did not survive. Glenn and Leonard Wood, who had fielded Fords and Mercurys with factory backing since the fifties, joined forces with David Pearson, forming a team destined to race into the NASCAR record books.

Backed by the Purolator Corporation, they campaigned a series of Mercury bodied cars. Pearson became the team's full-time driver in April, just before the Rebel 400, where he scored a convincing victory. He next won at Talladega in the Winston 500, and also won the Motor State 400, Fire-

Though Pearson's #21 Cyclone looked about as aerodynamic as a brick at first glance, it actually was one of the slipperiest GN race cars of its time. Built originally by Holman & Moody, the half chassis car featured a Galaxie frame member and suspension components at the bow and leaf sprung, unit body underpinnings at the rear.

Pearson's Cyclone packed a big wallop under the hood in the form of a race spec, Boss 429 engine. A cowl-inducted Holley Dominator kept the beast fed and cranking out in the neighborhood of 650hp. Speeds at Talladega with this topped 190. The Wood Brothers team later replaced Pearson's Boss motors with 427 Tunnel Port FEs when NASCAR restrictor plate rules had choked the Hemi nearly to death.

1971 MERCURY CYCLONE
Wheelbase: 115-118in
Weight: 3,800lb
Suspension: Screw jack-adjustable, reinforced
    control arms ('65 Galaxie or fully fabricated)
    and HD coils, twin shocks per wheel (front);
    HD screw jack-adjustable leaf springs, Ford
    9in differential with floating hubs, twin shocks
    per wheel (rear)
Brakes: Reinforced shoes/ventilated drums
Engine: 429ci, ohv, 1-4V, V-8 (Boss 429/hemi
    head), wet sump lubrication, 600-650hp
Transmission: Ford T&C, floor-shifted, four-
    speed manual
Speed at Darlington: 153mph

---

cracker 400, Yankee 400, and the Delaware 400. In 1972 Pearson was again in a '71 Cyclone and he won eleven of the eighteen races the team entered on a limited schedule. All told, Pearson and the Woods won seventeen of the thirty races they entered with their '71 Cyclone. Add to that record two superspeedway wins by A.J. Foyt in the Wood Brothers car.

Like the H&M '67 Fairlanes before it, Pearson's Mercury rolls on "big car" front suspension components and conventional Fomoco leaf springs aft. Power came from a variety of motors. Boss 429 hemis were used until they were choked with increasingly smaller restrictor plates. At that point, the cagey Wood Brothers campaigned the tried and true 427 Tunnel Port motors first developed for the 1967 season. Those long-out-of-production engines were still NASCAR "legal," and they were shackled with far larger restrictor plates than the big "Blue Crescent" Hemis. NASCAR based restrictor size on engine type in those days.

One of Pearson's Purolator Mercurys is on display at the Joe Weatherly Stock Car Museum in Darlington. It's an example of one of the last "half chassis" Fomoco stock cars to be campaigned.

RICHARD PETTY'S 1972 DODGE CHARGER

When Richard Petty got his Superbird's wings "clipped" by the NASCAR rules book in 1971, he first turned to a "stock" bodied '71 Road Runner as his high banks mount. Though he enjoyed great success in that car (twenty-one wins, $351,071 in winnings, and the season championship), late in 1972 Petty switched car companies and campaigned a new "Coke Bottle" bodied Dodge Charger. It was a move he never regretted. In fact, when asked to recall his favorite race car, Petty quickly mentions the sensuously shaped Chargers he campaigned from 1972 to 1978 (due to a long production run and NASCAR rules changes). These cars helped him win thirty-seven races, points titles in 1974 and 1975, and nearly $3 million.

Petty's Chargers were exceptionally good superspeedway cars, and in five seasons they won more than twenty high-banked events, including the pairs of Daytona 500s, Firecracker 400s, World 600s, and the 1974 Talladega 500.

In 1972 and 1973, Petty's Chargers used the venerable 426 Hemi for power. But when NASCAR turned a jaundiced eye toward the near-200mph speeds that engine

Richard Petty picked up STP sponsorship late in 1971 and represented that corporation until hanging up his driving gloves in 1992. The King's fleet of Coke Bottle bodied Chargers were arguably the most successful of all his STP red and Petty blue cars. They were built over a torsion bar and leaf spring chassis that had been fitted with reinforced front and rear chassis snouts.

Chryco engines for most of the preceding decade and a half, the King had to rely on small-block power for the last four years of his Chryco racing career.

His STP Charger was based on a unit body stamping mated to fabricated chassis snouts and fitted with torsion bar and leaf spring suspension components. After his return to Plymouth in 1970, Petty Engineering built the King's GN cars as well as most of the other Mopar cars on the circuit.

BOBBY ISAAC'S 1973 FORD TORINO

In the sixties, big was always better in the NASCAR ranks when it came to engine displacement. In fact, if not for a rules book stipulation that limited displacement to 430ci, drivers likely would have been flogging 500ci motors by 1969. NASCAR, however, had second thoughts about engine size as speeds at Talladega topped 200mph. Restrictor plates were introduced in 1970, and they became increasingly more restrictive as the decade progressed. But they were not

produced, Petty and his crew chief brother Maurice opted to run wedge-headed 426 engines like the one in the STP Dodge on display in the International Motorsports Hall of Fame in Talladega. In 1974 Petty spent $55,000 dollars of R&D money on a 358ci Mopar engine that NASCAR regarded more favorably. After fielding big-block

Like most NASCAR race cars, the control cabin in Petty's Charger is lacking in the ergonomics department. By the mid-seventies, fabricated racing seats were legal.

The 358ci Cleveland-powered Torino that Bud Moore built for Bobby Isaac in 1973 was the first small-block car on the modern day NASCAR circuit. In an era when 7-liter mountain motors were the dominant force, it was quite a risk to venture out on a NASCAR track with only 5.8 liters under the hood. Even so, Bud Moore and Bobby Isaac proved that the combination could work. Today, their pioneering effort has resulted in small-block Ford and Chevrolet engines being the only power plants that are currently legal for NASCAR competition.

quite as small for small-block engines—a fact not lost on innovative team owners like Spartanburg, South Carolina's Bud Moore.

When it became obvious that Ford's Boss 429 had been intentionally placed on NASCAR's endangered species list, Moore developed a viable small-block cased drivetrain. As it turns out, he was the ideal man for the job since he had two season's worth of small-block race experience as head of Ford's factory backed Boss 302 Trans-Am effort. Working with Ford's 351 Cleveland, cant-valved, small-block motor, Moore developed his own "mini-plenum" induction system and beefed up the engine's internals.

Installed in Bobby Isaac's '72 Torino, Moore's small-block produced about 500hp, enough to propel the car to second place in the 1973 Daytona 500. Isaac was running well in the Talladega 500 until—in one of the strangest happenings in

Like its street-going brothers, Unser's '72 Torino wasn't exactly the most aerodynamic automobile ever built. But that didn't really matter in road course competition. What counted there was horsepower and handling, and the Pepsi Cola backed car had more than enough of both to bring Unser home fourth in his first visit to Riverside.

NASCAR racing—he pulled into the pits at mid-race to announce his retirement. A lad named Darrell Waltrip got his first "name" ride when Moore tapped him to finish out the season.

Moore's white #15 Torino was built over a full chassis, a first for Fomoco race cars since the demise of full-sized Galaxies in 1966. Even so, it was fitted with a fabricated snout that retained the tried and true '65 Galaxie components many "rear steer" cars still use on the circuit today. Coils and trailing arms also appeared under the rear of a Ford racer for the first time in six racing seasons.

Bud Moore's #15 Torino currently belongs to Huntersville, North Carolina's Bill Bradford.

BOBBY UNSER'S 1972 TORINO

Ralph Moody and John Holman first met in the fifties when they were hired by Ford racing team chief Pete DePalo. Moody's mechanical genius coupled with Holman's administrative skill formed a winning combination. When DePalo left Ford, it was only natural for Holman & Moody to take his place as the head of Ford's NASCAR race effort. In the sixties, their Charlotte airport complex was a literal factory for racing, and all manner of race cars and race drivers passed through its doors. So pervasive was H&M influence and so innovative were their designs that most contemporary Winston Cup cars still carry at least a few (and in some cases, many)

Holman & Moody components, though that corporation has been defunct since 1974.

Unfortunately, Lee Iacocca's decision to strip Ford's racing budget to the bone in 1970 also cut the legs out from under H&M. By 1972, the sprawling complex that had once seen GT-40s parked next to Can-Am cars and GN stock cars was as quiet as a cemetery. The last H&M Grand National stock car ever built is shown here. It was built for USAC/Indy star Bobby Unser to campaign at the 1973 season opening road race at Riverside.

Powered by a full-tilt Boss 429 Hemi capable of cranking out more than 625hp, the car represented the cutting edge of NASCAR technology, circa 1973. Chassis components consisted of a modified factory frame fitted with H&M-developed suspension pieces fore and aft. It had drum brakes, transmission and differential coolers, and wet sump lubrication.

During the race itself Unser used his road course experience to manhandle the nose-heavy, 3,800lb car to a fourth place

H&M built their last race car with 429ci of Boss Hemi engine for power. The 625+ ponies it churned out were translated to the pavement through a screw jack-adjustable, coil spring suspension that is virtually identical to the set up still being campaigned under "rear steer" Winston Cup cars today.

Here's a rear quarter view of Unser's car. Inside, the cockpit of Unser's road course Torino was nearly as crowded as that of a current WC car. Both transmission and differential coolers competed for space with the dry sump reservoir, the onboard fire system, the bulk of the car's electricals, the roll cage, and, oh yes, Unser himself.

1972 TORINO
Wheelbase: 115-118in
Weight: 3,800lb
Suspension: Screw jack-adjustable, reinforced control arms ('65 Galaxie and fully fabricated) and HD coils, twin shocks per wheel (front); screw jack-adjustable HD coils, panhard rod, trailing arms, Ford 9in differential with floating hubs, twin shocks per wheel rear)
Engine: 429ci, ohv, 1-4V, V-8 (Boss 429/hemi head) wet sump lubrication, 600-650hp
Transmission: Ford T&C, floor-shifted, four-speed manual
Speed at Darlington: 153mph
Speed at Riverside: 110mph

finish in his rookie race on the fabled 2.62mi Riverside track.

When photographed, Unser's unrestored H&M Torino belonged to Pensacola, Florida's Mike Durhan.

DAVID PEARSON'S 1975 IMSA/NASCAR GT FORD TORINO

Look closely at the car pictured on these pages for it is without a doubt one of the most unusual "stock" cars ever built. Consider that this particular car was specifically built to run at night—long before Humpy Wheeler lit up Charlotte Motor Speedway. Then there's the fact that the car sports brake lights and headlights. And let's not overlook the Ford's really unusual-looking (even by Grand National standards) "stock" body work.

The car stems from Bill France's desire around 1975 to inject international sports car endurance competition with a taste of "good ol' boy" style stock car racing. He helped cook up a new NASCAR GT division for the 24 Hours of Daytona in 1976. Like all cars in Grand National competi-

Low and squat to the ground and dressed out with a full lighting package, the '75 Torino that finished first in class at the 1976 24 Hours of Daytona looks quite unlike any NASCAR "stock" car before or since. IMSA rules of the day allowed radical body modifications for cars in the NASCAR/GT category that would never have been permitted by Grand National tech inspectors.

tion, the new racing classification had to be based on two-door, ohv, V-8-powered sedans produced by one of the big three auto makers.

The car that Jack Bowsher and John Holman built to run at Daytona and LeMans is pictured here. It was based on a fully fabricated GN-style chassis that was nearly identical to the one developed by Holman & Moody for oval track racing. Galaxie-based front suspension components and massive GN-style drums were used up front, and another set of drums and a trailing arm-equipped, coil spring combination brought up the rear.

Power came from a dry sump-equipped Boss 429 engine mounted as low and rearward in the chassis as possible to aid handling. The car's mechanical components were covered in a "cheated up," cut-down version of a '75 Torino body shell. The Torino's body has been sectioned so severely that its rocker panels are completely missing. As a result, its red metalflake roofline barely rises above belt buckle level. Large front and rear spoilers add to the car's road

A Boss 429 was responsible for motivation. The 650-odd horsepower the engine produced moved the 3,500lb car with sufficient dispatch to blow off Greenwood Corvettes down Daytona's back stretch.

1975 IMSA/NASCAR GT FORD TORINO
Wheelbase: 115in
Weight: 3,500lb
Suspension: Screw jack-adjustable, HD coils and fabricated control arms, twin shocks per wheel, sway bar (front); screw jack-adjustable, HD coils, panhard rod, trailing arms, Ford 9in differential with floating hubs, twin shocks per wheel (rear)
Brakes: Reinforced shoes/ventilated drums
Engine: 429ci, ohv, hemispherically chambered, 1-4V, (Boss 429), V-8, 600- 650hp
Transmission: Ford T&C, floor-shifted, four-speed manual
Speed at Darlington: N/A

A team of drivers that included David Pearson took turns behind the wheel in this cramped cockpit during the 1976 running of the Daytona "Continental" 24-hour endurance race. One can only wonder what "tiddler" sporty car types thought when being overtaken by the 17ft long stock car.

race looks and serve as the mounting points for brake and driving lights.

David Pearson, his son Larry, and Jack Bowsher's sons, Gary and Jim, were signed to drive the car at Daytona. The two Pearsons piloted the car to a daytime lead in their class before surrendering the helm to the Bowsher brothers, who brought it home first in class and sixteenth overall; a very respectable showing considering that the Torino was sidelined for three full hours during the race while a blown motor was changed.

Plans to campaign the car at the fabled 24 Hours of LeMans fell through when John Holman unexpectedly passed away and the Torino never raced again. Today it belongs to Gastonia, South Carolina's Kim Haynes.

BOBBY ALLISON'S 1974 MATADOR

In the early seventies, American Motors Corporation (AMC) decided to venture into factory backed racing, and NASCAR's Grand National stock car circuit was one venue where trademark red, white, and blue AMCs did battle against cars from Detroit's "Big Three"—and not without success, we might add.

Roger Penske was the moving force behind AMC's first season of NASCAR competition in 1973. Holman & Moody built the first of a series of GN Matadors, and famed sports car driver Mark Donohue won the season-opening Winston Western 500 at Riverside. A big reason for the win was the disc brakes Penske fitted to the Matador's chassis—a first on the NASCAR circuit.

Bobby Allison got behind the wheel in 1974 and enjoyed real success with top five finishes in five of seven races entered and a victory in the season finale at Ontario. However, the win was spoiled somewhat by a record post-race fine of $9,100 for Penske's illegal installation of roller rocker arms (commonplace today on the circuit).

Allison started the 1975 season from the pole at Riverside and won the 500mi race, took second at the Daytona 500, and two starts later won again, this time at the Rebel 400 in Darlington. Mechanical gremlins plagued the car for the remainder of the season, and blown engines ended Allison's day prematurely at eight races.

Allison's last appearance in a Matador came in 1976 at the season-opening Riverside race. Engine failure sidelined the car on lap 149 of that race, the Western 500. Penske switched over to Mercurys at the Daytona 500 and never campaigned a red, white, and blue "Rambler" again. All told, Matadors started seventy-five GN races, sat on the pole four times, won four, and finished in the top five twenty times.

The Roger Penske-prepared Matadors were first built by Holman & Moody. Later versions were built by Allison in his Alabama fabrication shop. All featured front and rear chassis snouts and screw jack-adjustable, coil spring front suspensions. The cars that came out of Allison's shop carried Chevelle-based "front steer" spindles and related steering gear, and fully fabricated control arms. Conventional leaf springs and a Ford differential were used aft. Power for AMC's enviable, albeit short, racing record was provided by a 364ci version of the corporate V-8 that had been treated to racing modifications similar to those Penske used to win the Trans-Am championship for AMC in 1971. Those tricks produced upwards of 500hp, which

Though AMC products are not normally associated with NASCAR racing, for a three-season period during the seventies, Roger Penske proved that they could run with the best. His red, white, and blue GN stockers were all built around Matador sheet metal bodies and fabricated frames. The first cars in the fleet were constructed at Holman & Moody while later versions, such as this one, were built by Bobby Allison.

1974 MATADOR
Wheelbase: 115in
Weight: 3,800lb.
Suspension: Screw jack-adjustable, HD coils a nd fully fabricated (GM, front steer based) control arms, twin shocks per wheel, sway bar (front); HD leaves, Ford differential with floating hubs, twin shocks per wheel (rear)
Brakes: HD ventilated discs
Engine: 364ci, ohv, 1-4V, V-8, 514hp
Transmission: Borg Warner, floor-shifted, four-speed manual
Speed at Darlington: 153mph

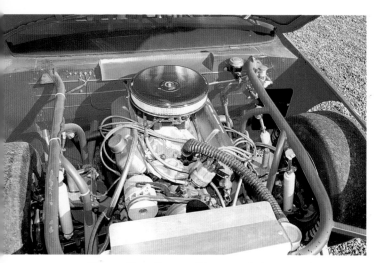

Roger Penske used many of the speed secrets he'd developed for his Trans-Am Javelins to wake up the AMC small-block engine. Though plagued with the "teething" problems common to any new racing effort, engines like this 364ci engine still produced enough power to win four Grand National races and score fifteen top five finishes.

were then handed off to a Borg Warner based four-speed transmission. The disc style brakes that Penske had introduced to the circuit in 1973 continued to prove the viability of that arrangement throughout Allison's tenure with the team. Today they are the industry standard.

An example of Allison's Penske Matador is currently on display at the International Motorsports Hall of Fame in Talladega.

RUSTY WALLACE'S 1980 CHEVROLET MONTE CARLO

Roger Penske has always had an eye for driving talent. Penske's first foray onto the NASCAR high banks struck pay dirt in the mid-seventies when Bobby Allison was signed to drive a team Matador.

Penske's return to the NASCAR ranks in 1980 was a success, too. Penske signed USAC rookie of the year Rusty Wallace for a "one shot" ride in the Atlanta 500. The 23-year-old Wallace finished that race just a tick less than 10 seconds (sec) behind an equally fresh-faced Dale Earnhardt, who scored his second career victory that day.

Wallace's mount in that first GN outing was Penske's #16 Norton-backed '80 Impala. Eight months later when Penske decided to field a car at a second 1980 NASCAR event, it was only natural for him to put Wallace behind the wheel. The race was the National 500 in Charlotte, and Wallace was behind the wheel of a blue and white Norton-backed '80 Monte Carlo. After qualifying twenty-fifth, Wallace turned in a solid performance but once again finished behind (in this case, fifteen positions behind) race winner Dale Earnhardt.

A reminder of their first pairing today belongs to Davidson, North Carolina's Alex Beam. The recently restored #16 Monte Carlo in Beam's impressive collection recalls both Wallace's first appearance on

1980 CHEVROLET MONTE CARLO
Wheelbase: 115in
Weight: 3,700lb
Suspension: Screw jack-adjustable, HD coils and fully fabricated control arms, twin shocks per wheel, sway bar (front); screw jack-adjustable, HD coils, panhard rod, trailing arms, Ford 9in differential with floating hubs, twin shocks per wheel (rear)
Brakes: HD ventilated discs
Engine: 358ci, ohv, 1-4V, V-8, 550-650hp
Transmission: Borg Warner Super T-10, floor-shifted, four-speed manual
Speed at Darlington: 153mph

1980 Monte Carlos were big as a house and anything but aerodynamic. Even so, they were standout race cars on NASCAR's short tracks because of their wide stance and stock engine setback (which produced a favorable center of gravity). Though the more aerodynamic Chevelles of the period might have gotten most of the glory due to their use on the superspeedways, it was the ungainly looking Monte Carlo that actually won the most races.

Right
The Monte Carlo's oddly bulging fenders actually worked well on NASCAR's short tracks because they provided a fair amount of crush room around the tires. Beneath those fenders was a fully fabricated frame that had been built up on a surface plate. Though there were Bow Ties all over the car's exterior, the whole package rolled on what was basically a '65 Galaxie suspension set-up.

the NASCAR circuit and the wide-tracked Monte Carlos that dominated GN competition in the late-seventies.

Wallace's car was built over a fully fabricated chassis clothed in skin that, for the most part, owed more to the fabricator than the assembly line worker. Holman & Moody suspension components evolved from the '65 Galaxie line were used at the bow, and a coil sprung trailing arm-located Ford differential was mounted aft. The powertrain was based on a race-prepped 358ci version of the familiar Chevrolet small-block engine, which produced somewhere around 500 race-ready horsepower.

DALE EARNHARDT'S 1977 OLDSMOBILE

After Dale Earnhardt's first Grand National race at Charlotte in 1975, there were probably few who suspected that he would become one of NASCAR's biggest superstars. Truth be known, his performance in Ed Negre's #8 '74 Dodge didn't really set the racing world on fire—unless you'd call finishing twenty-second, forty-five laps behind the leaders in the World 600 impressive. The next three seasons weren't much better. But in 1979, Earnhardt signed

Dale Earnhardt's first well-financed NASCAR ride was provided by West Coast racer Rod Osterland. In 1979 Earnhardt won Rookie of the Year honors in Osterland's blue and yellow #2 Chevrolets. He backed that performance up in 1980 with five wins, fourteen top five finishes, and the NASCAR driving championship—an unprecedented feat. This Olds is one of the cars he drove at Talladega that season.

Like all GM stock cars since the mid-seventies, Earnhardt's Oldsmobile was powered by a high-horsepower version of the Chevrolet small-block engine. NASCAR rules limit engine size to just 358ci. Even so, a skilled engine builder can extract upwards of 650hp from a "Mouse" motor slated for NASCAR competition. That was enough in 1980 to propel Earnhardt to just less than 200mph at Talladega.

1977 OLDSMOBILE
Wheelbase: 115in
Weight: 3,700lb
Suspension: Screw jack-adjustable, HD coils and fully fabricated control arms, twin shocks per wheel, sway bar (front); screw jack-adjustable HD coils, panhard rod, trailing arms, Ford 9in differential with floating hubs, twin shocks per wheel (rear)
Brakes: HD ventilated discs
Engine: 358ci, ohv, 1-4V, V-8, 550-650hp
Transmission: Borg Warner Super T-10, floor-shifted, four-speed
Speed at Darlington: 153mph

---

a contract with California team owner, Rod Osterland that led to his first championship. The rest, as they say, is history.

Earnhardt's first year in the Osterland-prepped #2 Chevrolet was an outstanding one. Twenty-seven starts produced his first GN victory (at Bristol in the Southeastern 500), eleven top five finishes, and the 1979 Rookie of the Year crown. Winning Rookie of the Year honors has proved to be the kiss of death for many NASCAR careers but Earnhardt was not one of the award winners who quickly faded into obscurity. In fact, in 1980 Earnhardt achieved the virtually impossible by winning the Winston Cup driving championship the year after he cinched top rookie honors. No one before or since has duplicated that performance.

That season he campaigned Osterland's yellow and blue Monte Carlos on short tracks and slope-nosed Oldsmobiles at Talladega. The "Intimidator" won five races that year, including big-track triumphs in the Atlanta 500 and the National 500. Those wins and fourteen other top five finishes helped Earnhardt win the championship by nineteen points ahead of Cale Yarborough. That, of course, would not be the last of Earnhardt's NASCAR driving titles.

Though it was a three-year-old bodystyle in 1980, the '77 Oldsmobile Cutlass was still that year's most aerodynamic car on the circuit. This was primarily due to the sloped angle of the car's nose as it rose from the front bumper. The angled rear backlight also helped contribute to fast back stretch speeds at Talladega. Earnhardt's first outing in the car came in the Winston 500 in May of 1980. David Pearson's Oldsmobile set a fast lap in qualifying of 197.704mph. Earnhardt's speed was good enough for a fourth place start. When the green flag fell, Earnhardt led the second lap and fifty subsequent circuits of the 2.66mi tri-oval. By the late stages of the race, Earnhardt's Olds was the dominant car on the track and he led twenty-nine of the event's last thirty-one laps. Buddy Baker, that year's Daytona 500 winner, passed Earnhardt with just three laps to go and was able to put the nose of his #28 Ranier Racing Cutlass over the finish line 3ft in front of Earnhardt's. The story was much the same in August at the Talladega 500. Earnhardt was leading late in the race until Neil Bonnett made the winning pass on lap 184. Cale Yarborough also slipped by and Earnhardt was third at the flag.

Like all modern NASCAR cars, Earnhardt's Osterland Olds was built over a tubular steel frame and rolled on fully fabricated suspension components fore and aft. Power was provided by a high-revving small-block Chevrolet engine breathing through a single four-barrel carburetor and a set of free-flowing, flat collector headers. When bolted into the Cutlass's aerodynamic body, speeds just short of 200mph were possible at Talladega.

One of the Mike Curb-sponsored Osterland Oldsmobiles that Earnhardt drove at Talladega belongs to Davidson, North Carolina's Alex Beam.

BILL ELLIOTT'S/DALE EARNHARDT'S 1982 FORD

The face of NASCAR racing changed in the early eighties. In 1981, new rules forced car builders to abandon the tried and true 115-118in wheelbase race cars that had been used since the early sixties. As wheelbase shrank so, too, did body size and aerodynamic profile. Fords of that era were changed the most. New, smaller Thunderbirds showed up as replacements for the block-long, full-sized Fords and Mercurys that teams like Bud Moore and the Wood Brothers had campaigned for nearly half a decade.

The faces of drivers also changed. Many stars of the sixties and early seventies had retired by the eighties and in their place were hungry young lions like Dale Earnhardt and Bill Elliott. Earnhardt and Elliott

Though it may come as a surprise to Dale Earnhardt's Chevrolet fans, he drove Ford Thunderbirds for team owner Bud Moore in 1982 and 1983. Earnhardt's downsized '82 Ford was built over a fully fabricated 110in wheelbase chassis identical in most ways to the one still being used on the circuit today.

Left
The Ford Motor Company was still officially on the NASCAR sidelines in 1982. As a result, high-performance Fomoco engine parts were becoming scarce. In fact, some teams had to go as far afield as Australia to find rebuildable blocks for their 351 Cleveland-based racing engines. When the "good stuff" could be found, a 358ci Ford motor of that era produced upwards of 500hp.

70

Bill Elliott had yet to pick up his "Awesome" nickname or win a race in 1982. Both would come in the next few seasons.

are most often thought of as arch rivals on the track. But in 1982 they were teammates of sorts—at least as far as brand loyalty was concerned. They both campaigned new downsized versions of the Ford Thunderbird that year. Earnhardt's car was prepared by famed team owner Bud Moore and carried Wrangler racing livery. Elliott campaigned a Melling-backed "Bird" that was maintained by his father and brothers in

their shop just outside of sleepy little Dawsonville, Georgia.

Both of their cars were built over fully fabricated, tubular frames that began life in Banjo Matthews' fabrication shop. Though shorter in length than previous NASCAR stock cars, the #9 and #15 Thunderbirds still used the same Galaxie-based suspension setups that had first been installed under Fred Lorenzen's Holman & Moody

Still racing for his family based race team that year, Elliott campaigned a boxy #9 Thunderbird like this one at twenty-one Winston Cup events. The eight top five finishes he scored were a hint of his promise as a driver.

1982 FORD
Wheelbase: 110in
Weight: 3,700lb
Suspension: Screw jack-adjustable HD coils, fully fabricated control arms, twin shocks per wheel, sway bar (front); screw jack-adjustable HD coils, panhard rod, trailing arms, Ford 9in differential with floating hubs, twin shocks per wheel (rear)
Brakes: HD ventilated discs
Engine: 358ci, ohv, 1-4V, V-8, 450-500hp
Transmission: Borg Warner Super T-10, floor-shifted, four-speed manual
Speed at Darlington: 155mph

1965 Galaxie. The two cars were also quite similar in terms of power. Both future NASCAR superstars relied on racing versions of the venerable Ford 351 Cleveland engine in 1982 for motivation. At the time, the 351 C had been out of production for a number of years, and with Ford still officially out of racing, parts were becoming scarce. With domestic high-performance components in short supply, Ford teams like Elliott's and Moore's had to go to extremes like importing used engine blocks from Australia (where 351 Cs were also

If you were to peek inside Earnhardt's car, you'd see that the cramped racing cockpits he and Elliott occupied in 1982 are nearly identical to their current race day workplaces. By the eighties the NASCAR rules book had so strengthened the racing roll cage that drivers commonly walked away from wrecks that would have been fatal in the sixties. Power steering, cool suits, and form-fitting, custom-built race seats all made Elliott and Earnhardt's "offices" more comfortable places to spend time.

used at one time). Ford's reentry to the factory sanctioned NASCAR ranks would help alleviate that problem one year later, but 1982 was still an underdog year for "Blue Oval" racers. Even so, both Elliott and Earnhardt ran well that season.

Both drivers remained with Ford in 1983, when the introduction of an all-new aerodynamic Thunderbird touched off a second round of factory backed aero wars. Earnhardt ultimately left Moore to drive Chevrolet race cars for Richard Childress.

73

Alex Beam of Davidson, North Carolina, owns these examples of Earnhardt and Elliott 1982 Thunderbirds.

BUDDY ARRINGTON'S 1985 DODGE

In the fifties, sixties, and seventies, Chrysler Corporation-based Grand National stock cars visited victory lanes 311 times and provided the vehicle for nine national driving championships. Lee Petty, his somewhat more famous son Richard, Tim Flock, Buck Baker, David Pearson, and Bobby Isaac were all crowned NASCAR champions after dominating seasons behind the wheels of Chryslers, Plymouths, or Dodges. The cars they drove included block-long Chrysler B300s, flat-back rooflined Chargers, Coke Bottle-bodied Chargers, radically winged Chargers, and boxy Belvederes. And who can forget the 426 Hemi engines that many of those cars were powered by, or the basso profundo symphony they produced while running away from the competition?

Buddy Arrington's boxy Dodge Mirada was the last Mopar stock car to date to run on a NASCAR Winston Cup track. After struggling with a diminishing parts supply and ever-increasing expenses for a number of years, Arrington parked his Mirada for good just before the spring Darlington race in 1985. Like all seventies vintage Chryco stock cars, Arrington's Mirada featured a torsion bar equipped fully fabricated frame. *Mike Slade*

1985 DODGE
Wheelbase: 110in
Weight: 3,700lb
Suspension: Adjustable torsion bars, fully
fabricated
    control arms, twin shocks per wheel (front);
    screw jack-adjustable, HD leaf springs, Ford
    9in differential with floating hubs, twin shocks
    per wheel (rear)
Brakes: HD ventilated discs
Engine: 358ci, ohv, 1-4V, V-8, 450-500hp
Transmission: Borg Warner Super T-10
Speed at Darlington: 156mph

Unfortunately, that mechanical music was muted when Chrysler closed down its motorsports operations shortly after a similar departure by arch rival Ford had made victory in the factory backed racing wars a moot point. Richard Petty soldiered on in his STP Dodge until August of 1978 before leaving the fold for Chevrolet. After the King's defection, only a handful of Mopar drivers continued to show the "flag" at tracks on the circuit. By the early eighties, long-time independent driver Buddy Arrington was the sole Mopar representative on the circuit.

Though Arrington had been a NASCAR regular since 1964, like many journeyman drivers, he'd never found a sponsor with deep enough pockets to properly fund a competitive race team. So, instead of finishing out in front, the Miradas Arrington built and prepared in his Virginia shop usually took the checkered flag far back in the pack. In the sixties that would have produced enough money in purses to sustain a frugal operation, but modern-era NASCAR racing is an incredibly expensive undertaking. In 1985, it became obvious that Arrington could not continue to campaign his

Dodge. The supply of race engines and chassis parts had all but dried up and the Mirada's boxy shape just wasn't built for speed. Four races into the 1985 season, Arrington reluctantly parked his #67 Dodge for good and switched to Ford. For the record, the last race featuring a Mopar stock car was the 1985 Coca-Cola 500 (nee Atlanta 500) in Hampton, Georgia. Arrington qualified thirty-second for that race and brought his Mirada home in eighteenth, thirteen laps down to winner Bill Elliott. Arrington's performance in his small-block-powered Dodge that day paid $5,855. It was the last money to be won to date by a Mopar driver on the NASCAR circuit. Arrington's Dodge is currently on display at the International Motorsports Hall of Fame in Talladega.

DALE EARNHARDT'S/DARRELL WALTRIP'S 1986 MONTE CARLO SS AERO COUPE

Chevrolet's Monte Carlo first saw NASCAR competition in the early seventies when Junior Johnson prepared a series of the new intermediates for drivers Charlie Glotzbach and Bobby Allison. For most of the rest of that decade and into the eighties, Monte Carlos were the most dominant race cars in the NASCAR series. That dominance ended in 1983, when Ford's new aerodynamic Thunderbirds were introduced. Recognizing the threat to the Monte Carlo's supremacy in advance, Chevrolet engineers introduced a new, sloping nose cone for the Monte Carlo line in 1983 that considerably decreased aerodynamic drag. Unfortunately, as slippery as that new beak was, it did nothing to improve the Monte

Dale Earnhardt won sixteen races and two Winston Cup championships while driving a Richard Childress-prepped Aero Coupe in 1986 and 1987. Their drooped snouts and bubble-backed rooflines bore a striking resemblance to the Torino Talladegas that

Ford used to dominate the very first factory aero wars in 1969 and 1970. Earnhardt's Monte Carlo was every bit as aerodynamic and successful as those first aero-variants had been.

Like all NASCAR cars of the modern era, "Iron Head's" Aero Coupe was built over a fully fabricated, tubular steel frame. Though the car's suspension components were primarily of Ford design, an all-Chevrolet drivetrain powered the car to victory.

Carlo's major aerodynamic flaw: a lift-producing, near-vertical backlight. At super-speedway velocities, air rushing over the roof of a Winston Cup Monte Carlo produced a dangerous amount of unwanted lift. And that's exactly what happened to Cale Yarborough's #28 Monte Carlo shortly after recording NASCAR's first official 200mph lap during qualifying for the Daytona 500 in 1983. Air tumbling off the roof just behind the backlight's precipitous plunge lifted the rear tires of Yarborough's orange and white car off the track and a horrendous, multi-flip accident resulted. Luckily, Yarborough

1986 MONTE CARLO SS AERO COUPE
Wheelbase: 110in
Weight: 3,700lb
Suspension: Screw jack-adjustable HD coils, fully fabricated control arms, single gas shock per wheel, sway bar (front); screw jack-adjustable, HD coils, panhard rod, trailing arms, Ford 9in differential with floating hubs, single gas shock per wheel (rear)
Brakes: HD Ventilated discs
Engine: 358ci, ohv, 1-4V, V-8, 600-650hp
Transmission: Borg Warner Super T-10, floor-shifted, four-speed manual
Speed at Darlington: 158mph

Dale Earnhardt and Darrell Waltrip used highly tuned evolutions of the venerable Chevrolet small-block engine to decide the Winston Cup Championship between themselves in 1986. Dressed in a single four-barrel carburetor and a set of stainless headers, a 1986 vintage 358ci mouse motor cranked out over 650hp.

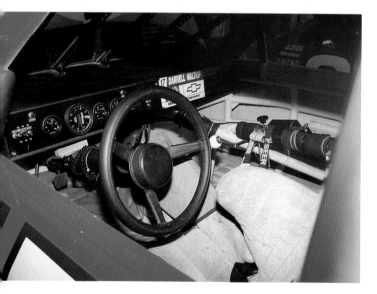

By 1986, the typical Winston Cup stock car's interior was a crowded affair. (Darrell Waltrip's is shown here.) A jungle gym's worth of roll cage tubing took up the most space. Other interior "appointments" included a custom-built racing bucket seat (outfitted with leg extensions), a quick-release steering wheel, a sophisticated on-board fire system, and a fabricated dash filled with a brace of analog gauges.

Right
1986 and 1987 were two of the last "unrestricted" seasons on the NASCAR circuit. Speeds those years at Talladega topped 212mph. The sloping, window and laid-down spoiler on Earnhardt's Aero Coupe helped make those incredible velocities possible.

Darrell Waltrip drove a Monte Carlo Aero Coupe for Junior Johnson in 1986. Like Earnhardt's similarly configured car, Waltrip's Chevy featured a drooped-snout and sloping roofline that allowed it to knife through the air on the superspeedways. Those aerodynamic add-ons helped Monte Carlo drivers break the 200mph barrier with regularity during the 1986 and 1987 seasons.

was uninjured and ultimately won the 500 in a Pontiac one week later.

Spurred by the increasing number of wins that Ford drivers were accumulating, Chevy engineers set out to solve the Monte Carlo's rear lift problem in 1986. Having already added a drooped and extended nose that closely approximated the beak Ford had used to create its all-conquering Talladega aero warriors in 1969, Chevy technicians built on that same theme by grafting on a bubble-back rear window that closely matched the Talladega's exaggerated fastback roofline. The new car was called the Monte Carlo SS Aero Coupe, and six-

teen of the forty-two cars in the field for the 1986 Daytona 500 were big-back-window Chevrolets. Geoff Bodine showed the car's potential by putting his #5 Aero Coupe on the outside pole and then driving to a convincing victory in the race.

Fellow Aero Coupe drivers Dale Earnhardt and Darrell Waltrip, followed Bodine's example in the races after Daytona, and in the process dominated the season driving championship. Earnhardt scored five wins and eleven top five finishes, and Waltrip took three checkered flags and recorded eighteen top five berths. Earnhardt won the Winston Cup championship,

Waltrip was second, and fellow Chevy driver Tim Richmond (who won seven races that year) was third. Earnhardt backed up his 1986 championship with another dominating performance in 1987.

All together, Monte Carlo Aero Coupe drivers won an incredible thirty-three of fifty-eight races contested in 1986 and 1987.

One of Earnhardt's Monte Carlos today belongs to Plant City, Florida's Bill Tower. An example of a Darrell Waltrip Aero Coupe has been restored by Davidson, North Carolina's Alex Beam.

BILL ELLIOTT'S 1987 THUNDERBIRD

Ford's jelly bean-shaped 1983 Thunderbirds were the first wave of a whole fleet of aerodynamic race cars that would ultimately rewrite the NASCAR record books. Their sleek, chiseled-by-the-wind styling was revolutionary both on and off the racetrack, and it worked. The period from 1983-1987 was characterized by ever-increasing speeds on the NASCAR circuit. As good as Ford's '83 to '86 Thunderbird was in terms of ultimate speed, the restyled T-Birds intro-

Though not readily apparent at the time, the line of redesigned Thunderbirds that Ford unveiled in 1987 were arguably the sleekest and most aerodynamically efficient NASCAR stock cars ever built. The Coors-Melling car that Elliott campaigned that year featured a snow plow-like front air dam, a gently sloping front hood and roofline, and a raised bustle that worked well in conjunction with a deck-mounted spoiler.

By 1987, the long dormant Ford Motor Company had awakened from its slumbers and was once again fully involved in stock car racing. The new head and engine castings that were supplied to racers in the mid-eighties greatly improved on the already powerful 351 Cleveland design that had first been harnessed for high bank duty by Bud Moore in 1972. In peak 1987 tune, engine builders like Ernie Elliott (shown here) and Robert Yates were extracting 650-675 reliable horsepower from the 5.8 liter engines.

Right
Ford redesigned the Thunderbird line for 1987. One small but significant change made to the car's basic silhouette was the raising of the rear deck lid. That alteration, combined with the installation of a more angled front facia, produced the fastest NASCAR race car of all time. Bill Elliott earned that title for Ford and Thunderbird at the May 1987 Winston 500 (nee Alabama 500) when he blistered the track with a qualifying lap of 212.809mph. That mark has never been broken.

Things got big in the windshield very fast indeed for Bill Elliott in 1987 when he was strapped into this racing cockpit. Notice the total lack of anything resembling a stock assembly line component. Save for hoods, trunks, and roof panels, modern Winston Cup race cars are built exclusively from fabricated or purpose-built racing pieces.

duced in 1987 were even better. In fact, it's likely that they will hold the record as the fastest NASCAR cars of all time for a good many years into the future.

Of all the Ford drivers to campaign Thunderbirds during the mid-eighties, Bill Elliott is without a doubt the most widely acclaimed. For a period of three years, his red, #9 Coors-Melling Thunderbirds were the fastest cars on the track. But it was the fleet of aerodynamic Fords that he fielded in 1987 that were fastest of all. In February of that year, Elliott scorched the track at Daytona with a 212.229mph qualifying lap

that was 7mph faster than his own pole winning speed of just one year before. Elliott translated that pole position berth into his second Daytona victory in three years. Two months later Elliott took the racing world's breath away with an all-time record 212.809mph lap during qualifying for the Winston 500 (nee Alabama 500).

Unfortunately, a potentially catastrophic shunt during that race put Bobby Allison's Buick nearly all the way through the grandstand fencing, injuring a score of spectators and red lighting the event for 2hr, 38min while injured fans and the mangled fence were attended to. The wreck gave NASCAR's attorneys pause to think about the legal consequences of a 3,700lb race car entering a crowded grandstand area at 200+ miles per hour. It also gave the sanctioning body a chance to do something about Elliott's lock on superspeedway glory.

Television coverage of the front-running #9 Thunderbird very seldom provided broadcast time for sponsors other than Coors (except as Elliott rocketed past lapped traffic, providing at least a fleeting glimpse of their commercial backers' logos). Truth be known, Elliott's ability to run away and hide from the competition (as he did in the 1985 Winston 500 where he lapped the entire field twice under green flag conditions!) on the superspeedways probably made NASCAR officials more than a little unhappy. Stock car racing circa 1987 had become a show (indeed, that's the very word racers use to describe what goes on out on the track) and, plainly speaking, a one-car show wasn't what most fans—other than Elliott's—wanted to see. It's also fairly certain that the folks in GM's front office (who had been there for NASCAR in the seventies after Fomoco and Chryco had pulled out of the series) were more than a little peeved.

Responding to pressure from all sides to trim speeds at Daytona and Talladega, the sanctioning body brought the dreaded restrictor plate (first used to clip Ford and Chryco's wings during the 1969-1970 aero wars) back from oblivion in 1988. The net result was a reined-in Bill Elliott, whose better-breathing Ford engine was more adversely affected by the plates than the 1955 design small-blocks used by his GM competitors. It also reduced terminal veloc-

1987 THUNDERBIRD
Wheelbase: 110in
Weight: 3,700lb
Suspension: Screw jack-adjustable, HD coils, fully fabricated control arms, single gas shock per wheel, sway bar (front); screw jack-adjustable, HD coils, panhard rod, trailing arms, Ford 9in differential with floating hubs, single gas shock per wheel (rear)
Brakes: HD ventilated discs
Engine: 358ci, ohv, 1-4V, V-8, 650-675hp (unrestricted)
Transmission: Borg Warner Super T-10, floor-shifted, four-speed manual
Speed at Darlington: 158mph

ities on the fastest tracks on the circuit. Those plates are still in use today and are the principal culprit behind the single file, freight train style of racing typical at Daytona and Talladega in the nineties.

Elliott's unfettered Thunderbird went on to win six races in 1987 and finish in the top five at sixteen others. At season's end he was second only to Dale Earnhardt in the championship points race. Ironically NASCAR's institution of the restrictor plate in 1988 did not prevent Elliott from winning his first Winston Cup Championship—the first for a Ford driver since 1969. With those flow-reducing below-carburetor plates still a fixture at Daytona and Talladega, and engine downsizing (to 5 liters) projected for the near future, it's likely that no one will ever surpass Elliott's 1987 superspeedway qualifying performance. That means that his 212.809mph Thunderbird is still, and perhaps will always be, the fastest NASCAR stock car in history. An example of an '87 Elliott T-Bird is currently on display at the International Motorsports Hall of Fame in Talladega.

THE CURRENT CHEVROLET LUMINA

Chevrolet has had a long and illustrious career on the NASCAR circuit. Since Herb Thomas scored the first Chevrolet triumph in 1955, Chevrolet NASCAR race cars have visited victory lanes more than 450 times since, more than any other manufacturer except Ford.

Dale Earnhardt, Darrell Waltrip, Bobby Allison, and Terry Labonte continued Chevrolet's winning ways in the eighties, winning all but one of the national driving championships contested from 1980-1989 in Chevrolets or Chevrolet-powered race cars.

The story has been much the same in the nineties. Earnhardt and his Chevrolet Lumina are still the combination to beat on just about any track on the circuit. That is, when other Lumina drivers aren't running at the front of the pack.

Sleek Chevrolet Luminas currently carry Chevrolet's corporate flag into "battle" on the NASCAR circuit. Trim and aerodynamically efficient, the Lumina is arguably the fastest Chevrolet NASCAR stock car ever built. Or, at least, it would be if not for the rules-mandated restrictor plate used at Daytona and Talladega.

Though the Chevrolet small-block has been around since 1955, it is still winning races today. A modern 18 degree-headed "mouse motor" is capable of cranking out somewhere in the neighborhood of 700hp. Restrictor plate engines produce 200 or so ponies less.

The cars that drivers like Earnhardt, Dale Jarrett, Darrell Waltrip, and a host of others currently campaign all started out as just an assortment of mild steel tubing and sheet metal stock on the surface plate of a race car fabricator's shop.

The completed chassis of a contemporary WC Lumina today usually rolls on a mixture of Chevrolet and Ford-based suspension components that are common to all cars on the circuit. Modern "front steer" cars, for example, use fabricated tubular front control arms that were derived from the Camaro line. Chevy truck-style trailing

CURRENT CHEVROLET LUMINA
Wheelbase: 110in
Weight: 3,500lb
Suspension: Screw jack-adjustable, HD coils and fabricated control arms, single gas shock per wheel, sway bar, (front); screw ack-adjustable, HD coils, panhard rod, trailing arms, Ford 9in differential with floating hubs, single gas shock per wheel (rear)
Brakes: HD rentilated discs
Engine: 358ci, ohv, 1-4V, V-8, 700hp
Transmission: Borg Warner Super T-10, floor-shifted, four-speed manual
Speed at Darlington: 159mph

arms and a Ford 9in differential, in contrast, are used at the rear.

A high-horsepower evolution of the familiar Chevrolet small-block is used to power a '94 Lumina, and can be relied upon to produce 700 or so unrestricted horsepower when a driver puts the hammer down. An aluminum-cased evolution of the Borg Warner T-10 transmits that power to the pavement through a track-specific set of gears in the Ford-evolved differential.

That potent package is housed in a sheet metal body that is far removed from the assembly line. Except for the hood skin, deck lid and roof panel, a modern WC Lumina carries a mostly hand-built body.

In race trim, a 1994 WC Lumina can clock 159mph velocities at Darlington. Saddling a free-revving small-block motor with a rules-mandated restrictor plate, however, trims power by a whopping 200 ponies. Modern Luminas are still so aerodynamically efficient that velocities over 195mph are possible at Daytona and Talladega.

THE CURRENT PONTIAC GRAND PRIX

Pontiac race cars recorded their first NASCAR win in 1957. By 1961, they were the dominant cars on the circuit. Marvin Panch won the Daytona 500 in a Smokey Yunick-prepped Poncho that year and Fireball Roberts made it two in a row for Pontiac in the 500 one year later in yet another Yunick-built Super Duty Catalina.

Darrell Waltrip, one of the most popular racers in NASCAR history, piloted this colorful Tide Lumina to several big victories.

89

CURRENT PONTIAC GRAND PRIX

Wheelbase: 110in

Weight: 3,500lb

Suspension: Screw jack-adjustable, HD coils, fully fabricated control arms, single gas shock per wheel, sway bar (front); screw jack-adjustable, HD coils, panhard rod, trailing arms, Ford 9in differential with floating hubs, single gas shock per wheel (rear)

Brakes: HD ventilated discs

Engine: 358ci, ohv, 1-4V, V-8, 700hp

Transmission: Borg Warner Super T-10, floor-shifted, four-speed manual

Speed at Darlington: 159mph

Contemporary Pontiac Grand Prix race cars look smooth and rounded from any angle. Those smooth edges along with the steeply raked wind screen and sloping front bodywork help the car slip through the wind with minimum resistance. Richard Petty switched to Pontiac Power in the early eighties. He finished out his illustrious, 200-victory career in a 1992 Grand Prix like this one.

GM's decision to terminate all of its divisions' motorsports activity in 1963 ended that streak.

It wasn't until 1981 that GM's "Indian Head" division once again visited a NASCAR winner's circle. Since that time, though, drivers like Richard Petty, his son Kyle, and Rusty Wallace have made Winston Cup Pontiacs a regular fixture at the head of the racing pack. It was, after all, a race spec Grand Prix that Wallace used to bully the competition on his way to the Winston Cup Championship. And who can forget the landmark 200th career victory that "King" Richard Petty scored in his STP LeMans as President Reagan looked on.

Aerodynamics is the secret behind Pontiac's recent success and it's not hard to understand why. The Grand Prixs are some of the sleekest stock cars ever built. Built over fully fabricated tubular steel frames, these Pontiacs feature wind tunnel-honed sheet metal silhouettes that cut through the air like a hot knife through butter. Interestingly, though quite stock looking from a distance, a modern Pontiac race car is actually almost completely constructed of flat sheet metal panels bent to shape on an English forming wheel.

Beneath that slippery skin is a drivetrain built around a Chevrolet small-block that is capable of propelling a race-ready Poncho to the far side of the double ton. A "Bow Tie" block serves as the foundation for all of that horsepower and it houses a high-compression 14:1 forged steel and aluminum reciprocating assembly. The engine has NASCAR-legal 18 degree heads (a term that refers to valve angle) and a high-rise, single-plane intake manifold mounted to the short block's deck surfaces. A dry sump oiling system is used to button up its "lower

Pontiac NASCAR cars have been motivated by versions of the GM small-block Chevrolet engine since the seventies. Modern engine builders are able to extract nearly 700hp from a mere 358ci. If the 421ci Super Duty engine that powered Fireball Roberts' Catalina in 1962 had received as much R&D work as the Chevy small-block, it would likely produce more than 1,000hp today!

tract." A 1 11/16in bore Holley carburetor and a set of flat collector, stainless steel headers complete the engine's underhood accoutrements. In peak tune, a race spec 358ci Chevrolet small-block is capable of producing nearly 700hp.

That estimable amount of power is transmitted to the racing tarmac through a racing chassis constructed of mild tubular steel. Fully fabricated front "A" frames, HD coils and a large-diameter sway bar are mounted to the front of the frame along with a Delco power-assisted steering box

and front steer drag link, tie rod assembly. Trailing arms, a panhard rod, and a pair of coil springs serve to locate the Ford 9in floater housing at the rear of the chassis. Massive, multi-piston, ventilated disc brakes, and gas charged shocks complete a modern Grand Prix's underpinnings.

THE CURRENT FORD THUNDERBIRD

NASCAR stock cars of the Fomoco persuasion have been winning races since the inaugural "strictly stock" event at Charlotte Speedway in 1949. In fact, Ford and Lincoln Mercury drivers have visited victory lane more than 450 times.

Today, Ford drivers like Mark Martin, Bill Elliott, and Geoff Bodine race into the future in aerodynamic Thunderbirds. Their 3,500lb Winston Cup stockers are hand-built silhouette cars that have been built over a tubular steel frame. Rear steer Thunderbirds still carry front suspension components based on the '65 Galaxie pieces developed by Holman & Moody, while front steer cars mount control arms evolved from the Camaro line. In either case, rear suspension components consist of a corporate 9in differential, located by a cross-chassis panhard rod and a pair of trailing arms

A modern Winston Cup Thunderbird is one of the sleekest stock cars ever built. Its rounded edges, angled windscreen and sloping roof line are all designed to slip through the air with a minimum of resistance. That slippery silhouette, when coupled with a high-horsepower small-block engine, makes triple-digit velocities just a stab of the gas pedal away.

One-piece plastic front and rear body caps
make the goals of body fabrication and
product identification much easier to achieve.
The front spoiler is like a snow plow. In the
rear, the dry break gas filler that makes the
typical 22 gallon fill-up a lightning fast affair.

CURRENT FORD THUNDERBIRD
Wheelbase: 110in
Weight: 3,500lb
Suspension: Screw jack-adjustable, HD coils,
    fully fabricated control arms, sway bar, single
    gas shock per wheel (front); screw jack
    adjustable, HD coils, trailing arms, panhard
    rod, Ford 9in differential with floating hubs,
    single gas shock per wheel (rear)
Brakes: HD ventilated discs
Engine: 358ci, ohv, 1-4V, V-8, 700hp
Transmission: Borg Warner Super T-10, floor-
    shifted, four-speed manual
Speed at Darlington: 159mph

borrowed from the GM truck lines. Massive four- or six-piston calipers act on ventilated discs that are mounted at all four corners to scrub off speed.

Power for a contemporary WC Thunderbird is cooked up by a racing evolution of the 351 Cleveland engine that Bud Moore first introduced to the circuit in 1972. These high-revving engines are built around a four-bolt main journaled SVO block and a forged steel SVO crank. Forged steel rods, forged aluminum 14:1 pistons, and a cobby roller camshaft are used to dress out the engine's short block. Robert Yates-developed, poly-angle valved, alloy heads working in concert with a single-plane, high-rise aluminum intake, and a dry sump oiling system makes the resulting rotation possible.

Current NASCAR rules limit Winston Cup cars to a single, 1 11/16in throttle bore and a four-barrel carburetor, and they outlaw any direct connection between the cowl and the air cleaner cover. The engine uses a set of stainless steel racing headers, and NASCAR cars run sans mufflers so engines produce a wonderful basso profundo roar. In peak tune, today's 358ci SVO engine can produce more than 700hp in unrestricted trim, so a sleek, 3,500lb Thunderbird could hit speeds in the 220mph range at tracks like Daytona and Talladega were it not for the rules-mandated use of horsepower-reducing restrictor plates.

Ford drivers like Bill Elliott and Mark Martin go to work in crowded "offices" like this one. A single form-fitting racing bucket and a full racing harness hold them securely in place behind a quick-release steering wheel and fabricated dash. Notice the multitude of roll cage bars that make a Winston Cup stock car one of the safest competition vehicles ever built.